COMPREHENSIVE EMERGENCY MANAGEMENT FOR LOCAL GOVERNMENTS

DEMYSTIFYING EMERGENCY PLANNING

JAMES A. GORDON

Published by
Rothstein Associates Inc.
Brookfield, Connecticut USA
www.rothstein.com

ISBN 1-931332-17-7

COMPREHENSIVE EMERGENCY MANAGEMENT FOR LOCAL GOVERNMENTS:
DEMYSTIFYING EMERGENCY PLANNING
By James A. Gordon

ISBN 1-931332-17-7

PUBLISHER
Philip Jan Rothstein, FBCI, President
The Rothstein Catalog On Disaster Recovery
Rothstein Associates Inc.
    4 Arapaho Road
Brookfield, Connecticut 0608-3104 USA
☎   203.740.7444
☎ 1-888.ROTHSTEin (888.768-4783)
203.740.7401 fax
www.rothstein.com
www.DisasterRecoveryBooks.com
info@rothstein.com

TABLE OF CONTENTS

FOREWORD

BY MELVYN MUSSON, FBCI, CBCP

The increasing number of natural hazard disaster that have occurred recently, coupled with the increased potential for terrorist acts in North America, have increased both the need and urgency for the provision of effective emergency management in both large and small communities. This is at a time when consideration of Comprehensive Emergency Management and the plans supporting emergency management programs continues to grow within the emergency management forums.

At the same time, funding for emergency management is often a problem, particularly in smaller communities. There is often a need to utilize whatever resources are already available without incurring major expenditure. Jim Gordon's book comes at an opportune time with a "how-to" format plus the availability of many documents within the book that can be used as shown or tailored to meet an agency's or organization's specific needs.

Mr. Gordon has also taken the opportunity to incorporate references between the sections of this book and the thirteen elements incorporated in NFPA 1600 - *Standard for Disaster/Emergency Management and Business Continuity Programs* (National Fire Protection Association, www.nfpa.org). NFPA 1600 is increasingly important in part because it is the basis of The Federal Emergency Management Agency's (FEMA, www.fema.gov) *Capability Assessment for Readiness* (CAR). CAR was developed initially for the State level, and was developed jointly with the National Emergency Management Association (NEMA, www.nemaweb.org). The NFPA 1600 Committee is now preparing a new edition of this vital standard, planned for release in 2004.

A similar assessment has now been developed for local emergency management agencies (*Local CAR*). Although developed for emergency management agencies, the principles incorporated in CAR can also be utilized in other sectors including the private sector. At the same time, health care organizations are already developing capability assessments for readiness within their organizations.

Another important consideration is that NFPA 1600 is not intended to be a "how-to" standard. As with other NFPA Standards, 1600 is a performance-based standard, i.e., it details what needs to be achieved. How the organization or agency goes about complying with what is needed is up to each organization or agency.

From an overall standpoint, whether NFPA 1600 becomes mandatory depends on its adoption at the Federal, State or Local level, or by its adoption by regulatory agencies in the public and private sectors. There is also a "back-door" way that compliance with NFPA 1600 may become mandated: the new NFPA Building Code, *Building Construction and Safety Code™* (NFPA 5000) includes reference to NFPA 1600. Therefore, adoption of NFPA 5000 by any agency, organization or company could necessitate compliance with NFPA 1600.

Irrespective of these different adoption considerations, it is recommended that all Emergency Managers consider the elements detailed in NFPA 1600. This is where the "how-to" format of this book will be of major assistance to emergency managers, particularly those from small or medium sized agencies. In addition, members of larger agencies may also find it valuable as a reference source and a "memory tickler." They may also find useful outlines and forms that they can adapt as they review their plans.

Mr. Gordon has done an excellent job in covering the many facets of a Comprehensive Emergency Management Program. He provides many plan outlines, action lists, forms and other sample documentation which will be useful to emergency managers as they develop or review their plans.

Melvyn Musson
Internal Audit - Business Continuity Planning
Edward Jones
St. Louis, Missouri, USA
October, 2002

MELVYN MUSSON, CBCP, FBCI, *is the Business Continuity Planning Manager for* **Edward Jones,** *a major financial institution headquartered in St. Louis, Missouri, USA. He is responsible for the firm's Business Continuity Plan covering locations in the United States, Canada and the United Kingdom. This requires considerable coordination with several emergency management agencies.*

Melvyn has over 35 years experience in Risk Management and Loss Control. For the past twenty years he has specialized in the areas of Emergency Management, Emergency Response, Crisis Management and Business Continuity Management.

Melvyn was one of the founders of the Disaster Recovery Institute International (www.dr.org) and played an integral role in the formation of the Business Continuity Institute (www.theBCI.org), based in the United Kingdom. He is also a charter member of the NFPA 1600 Technical Committee.

PREFACE

Post-September 11th, 2001:
A New Paradigm for Emergency Planning in North America

Since the first settlement of North America, communities have had to plan for emergencies. Those emergencies have never been trivial and often were catastrophically fatal. As North American society developed and technologies evolved, so too did the nature of the threats faced by communities. Crop failures, floods, fire and extreme weather still face our communities but the consequences are now more psychologically traumatizing than fatal. Unfortunately, it is now the routine use of advanced technology that results in many of the catastrophically fatal emergencies, such as air and rail crashes.

These seem to be accepted parts of modern society which are mitigated through engineering or downplayed with the use of statistics. On September 11th, 2001, however, a sinister new element to local government emergency planning was revealed that was so preposterous it seemingly could only be the idea of a Hollywood screenwriter. Yet it *was* real - and profoundly, permanently changed the sense of security taken for granted by North American society.

International terrorism had arrived in North America on an unfathomable scale. Previous acts of terrorism in North America, such as the release of a biological agent in a small Oregon town by a religious cult in the 1980s, the World Trade Center bombing of the early 1990s and the Oklahoma City bombing, were either of a limited scale or intent. While still garnering our attention, these seemed localized in terms of impact and effect and the perpetrators were readily addressed by thorough police work that has become the North American standard. People were killed and injured in these events with the latter example exacting a horrendous death toll and widespread psychological trauma. While these are without doubt unacceptable acts, the persons and motivation for such acts have been determined and justice exercised. These have been crimes that fit conveniently into our way of thinking that encapsulates the stages of the act and ends with closure.

September 11th, 2001 was very different in so many ways. While unimaginable amounts of investigative time and skill has revealed some of aspects of this crime, the underlying, fundamental reason for it and the lack of closure, not to mention the deaths and injuries perpetrated upon many families, have left this act incomprehensible for many. It is the reasons for this act, whatever they may exactly be and whether one supports them or not, that may see either an increase of instances of international terrorism in North America, or certainly prudent planning steps to prepare for such.

North America has largely been immune to international political issues disrupting domestic society. As an example, the aircraft hijackings of the 1970s were generally contained to Europe and the Middle East where the issues at stake were germane. The same can be said for the other Middle Eastern conflicts where the perpetrators of such acts affect the citizens directly associated with a government or one side or another.

September 11th, 2001 was symbolic as well as real, and represents a dangerous new turn in potential emergencies that face all sizes of local governments. In addition to natural hazards and technologically based emergencies, deliberate acts of terrorism and sabotage designed to produce casualties and/or massive infrastructure interruption must be added to the emergency planner's list of hazards. It is no longer sufficient just to plan for the unpredictable natural events or to anticipate the failure of our technological advances; one must now assess concentrations of people and critical infrastructure and services for vulnerability to intentional interference.

Of course, where intentional interference is planned, the perpetrator will be seeking maximum effect. As a result, all local governments must adopt this new paradigm as each has vulnerable water systems, critical transportation systems or concentrations of people (e.g., large office or residential buildings, sporting venues or market places) that may prove to be enticing targets upon which to make a point. Fundamental to such emergency planning is a very careful and deliberate process that will look at all aspects of that local government including its services, functions, facilities, location and citizenry. In general, it is only certain types of vulnerabilities that need to be identified and planned for, after which it simply becomes a matter of scale.

Three general directions could emerge from this event: a point has been made and North America will see no more acts of this nature; the desired effect was achieved and other similar, large-scale attacks will occur; or, perhaps given the heightened security at "large" targets, a sustained series of smaller-scale attacks, such as bombings or chemical/biological releases, may occur. The actual answer is unknown but recent history has shown that the price of being unprepared is far too high.

James A. Gordon
Kamloopse, British Columbia, Canada
October, 2002

How To Use
This Book

This book is intended to be a "how to" guide for the local government employee designated to be the Emergency Program Coordinator. While it may also serve as a reference handbook for reviewing certain components of local government emergency planning and management, its structure was purposefully crafted to be a self-study course in assembling a Comprehensive Emergency Management Plan for a local government.

This book will find use in a wide variety of applications outside of the traditional model of North American local government emergency planning and management. The principles and processes presented are such that they will find application in urban and regional settings worldwide regardless of the actual local, regional, state/province or national government presence or role. Non-governmental agencies and not-for-profit organizations anywhere in the world will also find the principles and processes presented herein useful when working with different levels of government.

The fact remains that where concentrations of people require protection from potential hazards and a level of government or aid agency is motivated to act in this regard, this book will provide the step-by-step approach towards attaining comprehensive emergency management, or parts thereof where specific or partial planning is all that is needed.

Comprehensive Emergency Management has two aspects which are seamlessly incorporated into this book: preparedness planning and actual emergency management. Following through the chapters towards compiling a Comprehensive Emergency Management Plan takes the Emergency Program Coordinator (a term used here to convey more of a role than just "emergency planner") through mitigation efforts to avoid potential hazards or to accept and fully understand those which cannot be avoided; through the development of a Preparedness Plan that includes a hierarchy of different plans; and, to response and recovery issues that may not necessarily be "plans" *per se.* These are topics that need to be well thought through in advance to give effect to successful execution of the overall response and recovery effort. Examples include mutual aid agreements, staff and facility preparedness, public education, training and exercises.

Within this framework of Comprehensive Emergency Management, the approach presented in this book to the actual creation of emergency plans is modular in nature.

This approach sees the different types of emergency plans prioritized so that the basic elements are in place before more specific or lower priority plans distract the planning effort. It starts with the Preparedness Plan whose core is the Emergency Management Plan. The Emergency Management Plan is essentially the establishment and function of the Emergency Operations Center that is central to *any* emergency. Beyond this other plans may be called upon as needed with four identified as quite common:

- Emergency Social Services
- Emergency Public Information
- Emergency Telecommunications; and,
- Evacuation.

Also, hazard-specific preparedness plans can be created in accordance with a prioritized list of hazards facing a community. These allow for effective and efficient response when an emergency occurs. Certain Recovery Plans can then be focused on, such as a Service Continuation Plan.

This modular approach lends itself nicely to an effective step-by-step guide for non-experts in the field of emergency planning and management. It is intended to show that small to mid-sized local governments can put into place thorough and complete emergency plans with the minimal expenditure of resources. The biggest expenditure is in staff time, as expertise in the different areas of local government management need to contribute in various ways to the completion of the Plan. This element transcends the simple expenditure of resources as it is the commitment of time and effort that is prerequisite to undertaking and completing an endeavour such as this. Thus, support must be secured to embark on this journey, otherwise the complete and most meaningful application of this book will not be achieved.

To aid in this planning task, checklists, summaries, plan outlines and a glossary are provided as helpful tools. In addition, appendices list resources available on the Internet that may helpful to the Emergency Program Coordinator in a specific area, and comments on the role and certification of professional emergency managers for those interested in pursuing professional development and formal recognition.

It is recommended, therefore, that the person undertaking the planning task read through the entire book to gain a complete understanding of the process and the philosophy. One can then go back to either start the process with tasks identified in the mitigation chapter, or to specific chapters that may be lacking in an existing plan. The local government undertaking Comprehensive Emergency Management for the first time can rest assured that following the steps contained in this book will result in a complete, relevant, useful and reliable Comprehensive Emergency Management Plan of which the community can be proud.

INTRODUCTION

A local government is formed when residents of a jurisdiction determine there is a need for a particular service, or set of services, which is either best provided to a group through an economy of scale rather than to an individual, or require the collective assets of a group (i.e., taxation), in order to finance that service provision. From such a humble start, local governments grow into extremely large and complex corporate entities with responsibilities for a vast array of services that cover large urban areas. The results of this evolution even in the most typical of small towns is that residents come to rely on the continued provision of these services, some of which are more critical than others, and that their urban area will remain safe for the free and unencumbered movement that we all expect.

It is not surprising to learn that our modern society has become a complex yet fragile web. At the macro level, our regions may be susceptible to potentially devastating weather phenomena, our cities and towns may be situated such that they are prone to site-specific natural events such as floods, avalanches, earthquakes and volcanic activity, while within the urban area the complex weave of infrastructure, transportation corridors and industry pose a daily risk of a highly disruptive event through technical or human failure.

This vulnerability at multiple levels would have impacts of varying scales. It is because of this likelihood that "anything happening at any time" that local government must plan for emergencies to occur and have readily available and well-practised preparedness plans available. Planning for the unexpected will ensure the maintenance of law and order, save lives, protect the health and welfare of residents and preserve property and the environment.

PURPOSE

The purpose of this document is to provide guidelines for the development of a Comprehensive Emergency Management Plan by local governments. In doing so it is hoped to achieve two objectives: to provide sufficient information to impart a basic yet broad understanding of the principles of emergency planning; and, to provide the necessary checklists and generally accepted practices where it is safe to generalize. Embarking on the task of creating an emergency plan, the planner must realize that each plan for each local government will be unique and require individual analysis and assessment, hence the need to understand the basic concepts rather than simply copying successful and proven plans from elsewhere. To the extent possible, common information and checklists will be provided to simplify the difficult task of *Comprehensive Emergency Management.*

Comprehensive Emergency Management is intended to provide the local government with the necessary plans which will aid in preparing for, responding to, and recovering from an emergency. Such steps will greatly aid in ensuring effective operation and corporate management of the local government since its responsibilities will continue in the event of extraordinary emergency situations.

CONTEXT

This document is intended to apply to those bodies who classify themselves as "local governments." The very general definition of a local government can be considered as that level of government which is responsible for the provision of one or more services directly to residents of a defined, yet geographically limited, jurisdiction. In Canada this can be considered to include certain kinds of service areas or improvement districts, municipal corporations and regional districts, whereas in the United States it can include municipalities and counties.

This document will rely heavily on the Canadian context and the British Columbia experience specifically. Illustrations from these areas will be used with the intent being to convey an important point which may then need further investigation within one's own jurisdiction. Principles in *Comprehensive Emergency Management* are universal and this work will endeavour to convey an emergency planning exercise which is widely applicable to Canada, the United States and internationally. This work will also find application in the private sector, with some modification, as well as with non-governmental organizations or international aid agencies consulting with all levels of government.

DEFINITIONS

The literature in this field appears to use "emergency" and "disaster" interchangeably and to the confusion of non-experts who generally find themselves as the emergency planner in most small to medium-sized local governments. Enrico Quarantelli, an authority on this subject at the University of Delaware, has stated that a disaster is not just a big emergency: that a disaster disrupts the entire social structure of a community, causing death, damage and destruction[1]. While this is an important definition of what may occur, it is perhaps more aptly used after an event to descriptively summarize what has occurred.

Conversely, the use of the term "emergency" more accurately describes the "operating mode" of those involved with a particular event while also covering the range of magnitude an emergency can take on from small-scale to large-scale.

This work will use the term "emergency" throughout for the sole purpose that it more appropriately conveys the point that emergency plans are not to be reserved for catastrophic events, rather that they may be called upon any time the highly organized, rapid decision-making capability enabled by a Comprehensive Emergency Management Plan and Emergency Operations Center is required. To this end, an "emergency" is defined as any present or imminent event that is caused by accident, fire, explosion or technical failure, or by the forces of nature, and requires prompt coordination of action or special regulation of persons or property to protect the health, safety or welfare of people or to limit damage to property[2].

SYNTHESIS

This work is a synthesis of current literature in this field and is supplemented by a distillation of the author's training and experience in emergency planning at two levels of government. Several areas of specific expertise, such as service continuation planning, have been incorporated as sub-topics under a larger, generic planning and management framework. The relevant principles of these specific areas have been placed in certain sections throughout this work to provide a logical sequence to the development of Comprehensive Emergency Management Planning by non-experts in the field of emergency planning.

IMPETUS

The motivation to put this work together was a frustration with trying to decipher a number of competing emergency planning paradigms taught at different levels of government. At senior levels of government, a military-like planning and operations mindset has dominated thinking for decades. After attending numerous emergency planning courses and years of frustration attempting to implement such models at the local government level, it has become clear that a new approach was required. Increasingly private sector thinking has been working its way into local government management over the last decade and many lessons in efficient, practical management can be learned from this sector. Large parts of the concepts in this book are taken from the private sector to hopefully yield a usable and very practical approach to local government emergency planning.

Another reason for putting this work together was to provide an easy to follow guide for the municipal staff member appointed as the Emergency Program Coordinator. Generally, the questions asked are, "What do I do?", and, "Where do I get some help?" This book is intended to be that help. All too often, local governments let pricey contracts to costly consultants to demystify emergency planning and to produce a large, complex and difficult to understand emergency plan which, usually, is of the old school of military-like thinking. This book will hopefully show that developing a Comprehensive Emergency Management Plan does not have to be time-consuming or overly complex. It is a guide, used personally, to develop thorough, realistic plans which address the needs of the community. The product will be concise, easy to follow and easy to employ. The target of this book is small to medium-sized communities with limited resources; however, the basics of any sound plan are encompassed here and may be expanded upon locally to develop custom local government emergency plans of a range of complexities.

NFPA 1600: STANDARD FOR DISASTER/EMERGENCY MANAGEMENT AND BUSINESS CONTINUITY PROGRAMS

No book or essay on any aspect of Comprehensive Emergency Management written today can overlook NFPA 1600 - *Standard on Disaster/Emergency Management and Business Continuity Programs* (referred to as "NFPA 1600").

The National Fire Protection Association (NFPA, www.nfpa.org) is an international organization which establishes codes and standards covering almost all aspects of emergency management. NFPA 1600 has its roots in 1991 when a committee was formed to develop guidelines for disaster preparedness, response and recovery. This resulted in the first edition of NFPA 1600 in 1995, entitled *Recommended Practice for Disaster Management*.

For the 2000 edition of NFPA 1600, this committee recognized the need for a more complete standard, and adopted a "total program approach" which greatly broadened the subject matter contained in the standard. This edition was entitled *Standard for Disaster/Emergency Management and Business Continuity Programs*. It expands upon preparedness, response and recovery to include general emergency program management and business continuity, in order to give a more complete coverage to the entire spectrum of preparation for, response to, and recovery from an emergency.

The 2000 edition of NFPA 1600 was approved by the American National Standards Institute (ANSI) and is endorsed in the United States by the Federal Emergency Management Agency (FEMA), the National Emergency Management Association (NEMA), and the International Association of Emergency Managers (IAEM).

The committee is now preparing a new edition for release in 2004. While called a "standard," it is still only a recommended standard which public or private enterprises may adopt; however, it may become a true mandatory standard in the near future. Regardless, it identifies critical areas of concern in developing and managing an emergency management program which any organization should adopt and from which they gain a certain degree of resilience.

This book was developed independently of NFPA 1600 in 2001 and 2002. The unique circumstances which prompted the writing of this book are identified earlier in this introduction. Specifically focusing on the needs of small to mid-sized local governments in developing and managing a comprehensive emergency management program has resulted in a remarkable parallel to NFPA 1600. In this book, I have attempted to go beyond the wise and insightful direction of NFPA 1600 by offering practical, "how-to" advice specifically written for the local government emergency planner.

Upon comparison of the two documents, it appears that the same material is covered but organized slightly different. This book is intended to walk the emergency planner through the complete process in more of a "guidebook" fashion rather than as a complete and useful reference manual I believe NFPA 1600 to be. Recognizing the growing importance of NFPA 1600 and as a means of providing a cross-reference to that document, the following paragraphs identify the NFPA 1600 sections covered in this book.

While this book is intended to be a complete guide for the local government emergency planner, those wanting to read further or seek a different description of a particular subject will find the following paragraphs enlightening.

- Chapter 2 of NFPA 1600 contains information relating to program management, specifically the establishment of a program planning committee; the position of program coordinator; program policy; and, assessment. These topics can be found in this book in Chapter 1: *Local Government Emergency Planning* under the subheading "*Who Does the Planning*" where the roles of the Emergency Program Planning Committee and the Emergency Program Coordinator are identified and discussed. In addition, the continuing responsibilities of the committee and the coordinator are discussed in Chapter 6: *Putting It All Together*.
- Chapter 3 of NFPA 1600 covers program elements in thirteen subsections:
  - *Laws and Authorities* are discussed in chapter 1 of this book under "Legislative Requirement" and "Authority." It is here where any statutory obligations to have an emergency program would be identified and then how this requirement is translated into an actionable basis for undertaking an emergency program. The NFPA 1600 standard discuses "industry codes of practice" which are specifically not addressed in this book (see *Impetus* in the Introduction chapter).
  - *Hazard Identification and Risk Assessment* is covered under Chapter 2: *Mitigation*. The subheading "*Risk Assessment*" includes a section on hazard identification which touches on internal and external hazards and developing a hazard inventory. Another subheading, "*Vulnerability Analysis*," touches on impact assessment.
  - *Hazard Mitigation* and *Resource Management* can also be found in the *Mitigation* chapter. Under the subheading "*Risk Management*" the four types of loss are discussed in addition to a five-step risk management process. The intent of this process is the elimination or minimizing of loss to the organization.

o *Planning* contains a number of sub-components which are covered under the *Preparedness* chapter of this book which discusses the emergency management spectrum and the structure of the Preparedness Plan:

- *Strategic Plan* - The equivalent of this plan would be found in the Emergency Management Plan. This is the crisis management framework which enables the local government to respond to an emergency.
- *Emergency Operations Plan* - These considerations are included under the Emergency Management Plan mentioned above, in particular the activation and role of the emergency operations center. Portions of this emergency operations plan, such as the deployment of key resources and the coordinated response to a specific situation, are also found in hazard-specific preparedness plans which are part of the overall Preparedness Plan.
- *Mitigation Plan* - The content of this plan is covered in the *Mitigation* chapter under the subheading "*Risk Management*" where the five-step risk management process is discussed.
- *Business Impact Analysis* - This analysis is included in the *Recovery* chapter where a detailed Service Continuation Plan is developed covering critical service functions, impact analysis and recovery issues.
- *Recovery/Business Continuation Plan* - These related topics are covered under the *Recovery* chapter. Specifically, the business continuation plan is covered under the "*Service Continuation Plan*" as noted above. In addition to this plan, this chapter includes pre- and post-emergency planning for facilities, staff and any special resources.

o *Direction, Control and Coordination* can be found in several sections of the *Preparedness* chapter. The management of response and recovery operations is addressed in the section detailing the Emergency Management Plan. This section covers the management of emergencies in a generic way as it may apply to a broad range of emergencies. Specific detail with respect to response and recovery management as it applies in the case of a specific emergency can be found in the hazard-specific preparedness plans. Likewise, the notification of staff and volunteers required under the deployment of any particular plan is covered under that particular preparedness plan.

o *Communications and Warning* can be found dispersed among the various plans that comprise the Preparedness Plan, as in the preceding paragraph. The establishment and testing of communications systems and procedures as they relate to the callout of staff and volunteers under a particular plan is included as an integral part of each plan. Communications systems in the larger sense of supporting the flow of dialog and decisions is found in the *Emergency Telecommunications Plan*. The exercising of individual plans, or specific sub-components thereof, is discussed in detail in the final chapter, entitled *Putting It All Together*. Here the different types of exercises are discussed, identifying the advantages and disadvantages of each.

- *Operations and Procedure* deals with tactical operations at the incident. This topic has been excluded from this book as management of the scene is considered the exclusive purview of the Incident Commander. He may direct the scene of the incident as he sees fit with any major tactical decisions taken relayed back to the EOC. The EOC serves the function of supporting the Incident Commander or coordinating resources if there are multiple incidents. Incident command is a skill of senior emergency services personnel covered under specific training courses. As such, it is beyond the scope of this book.

- *Logistics and Facilities* are generally covered in the chapter on *Response*. This chapter deals with emergency social services, of which one aspect is providing support for the incident (e.g., food and location/materials for rest and personal hygiene). This chapter also addresses mutual aid, where supplementary resources and personnel are required from neighboring local governments, and specialized equipment which addresses unique items that may be called upon during a response. Further details of unique requirements in terms of personnel, resources or other support are noted in the pertinent hazard-specific plan.

- *Training* is addressed in Chapter 6: *Putting it All Together*. Specifically, sections on general awareness education of potential emergencies as well as training requirements for responders are discussed. A training matrix is proposed for tracking the level of training required by all players in emergency response, as a method of differentiating those requiring increasingly advanced training for senior emergency management positions.

- *Exercises, Evaluations & Corrective Actions* can also be found in Chapter 6 under the subsection entitled *Exercising the Plan*. A detailed discussion of the various types of exercises is presented so that the appropriate type can be selected to best test a particular plan. Also, the benefit of thorough and impartial evaluation of exercises is identified as an important element. In addition, each plan suggested in this book carries a section committing it to an annual review with the intention of attempting to keep it current in terms of policy, procedures and staff turnover.

- *Crisis Communications, Public Education and Information* are addressed in Chapter 3: *Preparedness*. Specifically, effective and timely emergency public information is a commitment recommended to be specifically identified in the Emergency Management Plan. The corollary of this is the Emergency Public Information Plan which is intended to be a complete plan that includes providing useful information to citizens as well as addressing the unique requirements of media relations.

- *Finance and Administration* are generally dealt with in the "Authority" subsection of Chapter 1: *Local Government Emergency Planning*. While this section limits itself to the establishment and identification of program management and the necessary oversight, it does not develop prescriptive administrative or financial procedures, instead allowing the degree of control in these two areas to develop in accordance with local needs.

Hopefully this brief discussion of the interrelatedness of NFPA 1600 and this book will prove useful to the inquisitive reader. Some topics may be discussed in differing degrees of detail and obviously organized differently to meet different purposes. Both make excellent and complementary references for the emergency planner.

---

[1] Wilson, B. 1988. *City of Edmonton: An Emergency Plan That Works*. Emergency Preparedness Digest. July/Sept.

[2] Justice Institute of British Columbia. 1993. A Guide to the New Emergency Program Act.

1

LOCAL GOVERNMENT EMERGENCY PLANNING

> *Prior to undertaking the emergency planning exercise, an understanding of the basic concepts behind local government emergency planning must be gained. The generic planning process, Concept of Operation and the four phases of Comprehensive Emergency Management will be introduced. Finally, the ability to see the local emergency plan in the larger regional/county/state/province context will complete an exposure to the nature of local government emergency planning.*

BASIC CONCEPTS AND CRITICAL ELEMENTS

When an emergency occurs, the local government is usually the first to become aware of it and often mounts the first attempt to deal with it. Most provinces and states view local government as the "first line of response" in emergency situations with provincial or state resources only being dedicated to the effort when local resources are no longer capable of addressing the scale of the emergency.

In light of this view, it is prudent management for the local government to have a practical, workable, thorough, known and understood Comprehensive Emergency Management Plan. In deed, in some provinces and states it is mandatory that local governments have emergency plans to ensure that the initial local effort is a planned and realistic response.

It is an unrealistic position for a local government to assume either emergencies of an escalating or unmanageable scale will not happen within one's boundaries or that county, state or provincial resources will be used in an initial response (unless previously contracted to do so). Thus, a discussion of the peculiarities of emergency planning at the local level is in order.

LEGISLATIVE REQUIREMENT

While an emergency plan is prudent management on the part of local governments, for it to be meaningful local governments must have access to, or be empowered with, special powers when an emergency is declared. Such powers typically include the ability to expend funds without the standard checks of routine expenditures, the ability to commandeer equipment and resources and the ability to restrict the movement of its residents or to order evacuations.

Such powers are not, and indeed should not be, entrusted to local governments on a permanent, on-going basis. These powers are usually invoked when a *state of local emergency* is declared. Powers at the provincial or state level, usually resting with the Attorney General, can be delegated to the local government when a state of local emergency has been declared by following a specified procedure. This procedure is usually the final and ultimate phase of executing the Comprehensive Emergency Management Plan. A requirement for a Comprehensive Emergency Management Plan forces local governments to confront and accept certain risks and hazards, to assess the threat and plan accordingly, usually enabling local governments to deal with the majority of eventualities.

In British Columbia, for example, the 1996 Emergency Program Act specifically requires all local governments to prepare municipal emergency plans. This Act provides for the local government to declare a state of local emergency after meeting specific criteria at which time substantial powers of the Attorney General transfer to the local government. Such responsibility is not to be taken lightly and when this measure is exercised, very close oversight is exercised by the Attorney General's office.

Local governments must research and understand the basic enabling legislation in their province, state or country. This not only provides the source of extraordinary powers and the criteria for their use, but also allows the Comprehensive Emergency Management Plan to be placed in the proper regional context so that local governments know what is expected of them should an emergency arise.

SENIOR LEVEL ENDORSEMENT

Meaningful and effective emergency plans at the local government level require the endorsement and active support at the most senior levels of municipal management. This will help in ensuring that senior managers understand their role in the plan, that staff support will occur throughout the organization and that sufficient funding and resources are made available.

The initial approach must be made to Council who must have their responsibility for public safety and preparedness impressed upon them. In some cases elected officials initiate the planning process after a poorly anticipated or responded to emergency, or information sessions by provincial or state officials. Council can make emergency planning a priority until a satisfactory plan is in place. With this support it will be easier to convince senior mangers to devote some time to participating in the planning process and making time for the necessary exercises.

A local government emergency plan is the tool senior managers will rely on for rapid coordination and decision-making in the event of an extraordinary situation. It is in their best interest to actively participate and this challenge falls to the Emergency Program Coordinator, for without this support the plan is all but useless. Participation in its development, a comprehensive understanding of the entire scope of the plan and periodic exercises to ensure some degree of retention are critical aspects. With the support of this group, it behoves the Emergency Program Coordinator to fully capitalize on it with a comprehensive planning process. This planning process will be investigated in detail.

AUTHORITY

The legislative requirement for local governments to have emergency plans must be translated through the means by which local governments operate. Specifically, in Canadian provinces this is a bylaw and, in the United States, it is an ordinance.

The purpose of a bylaw or ordinance is to put in place the formal direction the local government Council chooses to embark upon with the establishment of a municipal emergency program. It provides for the governance and oversight of the emergency program, the establishment of a position to coordinate or manage the program, the scope of the planning endeavour and any annual reporting requirements. This then provides the authority for the Emergency Program Coordinator to devote the necessary resources toward the objective of putting in place a workable and effective emergency plan. It also provides for certain critical aspects of the Comprehensive Emergency Management Plan such as the authorization for invoking the plan, a line of succession for the role of Emergency Program Coordinator, the role of Council, and the expected interaction between the Coordinator, the Emergency Program Planning Committee and elected officials.

Further, the bylaw or ordinance serves the legal function of demonstrating the local government's intent to fulfil the legislative requirement placed upon it. As well it reflects the extent of preparedness the local government is willing to go to as determined by the Council representing the community's residents.

WHO DOES THE PLANNING?

The instrument establishing local authority and direction for *Comprehensive Emergency Management*, specifically a bylaw or ordinance, should provide for two critical aspects of the local emergency program: an Emergency Program Planning Committee and an Emergency Program Coordinator.

EMERGENCY PROGRAM PLANNING COMMITTEE

The Emergency Program Planning Committee is the administrative body responsible for the preparation of the municipal emergency plan and subsequent reviews and amendments as necessary. It is a standing committee which is usually comprised of the following persons:

- a member of council
- municipal Chief Administrative Officer
- Emergency Program Coordinator
- Fire Chief
- Police Chief
- Chief Medical Officer or hospital/ambulance representative
- municipal Public Works Manager
- Emergency Social Services Director
- municipal Telecommunications Coordinator

Other representatives may be added as necessary in order to achieve the general planning goals of the committee or a specific planning objective. Sub-committees may be formed to develop hazard-specific preparedness plans which may include specific experts not listed here such as utility, transportation and industry representatives.

Its primary function is to provide guidance to the Coordinator. While the Coordinator facilitates the wishes of the Committee, the Committee in turn sets the direction of the program which the Coordinator, as the dedicated resource on either a full-time or part-time basis, researches, writes and executes. The Committee should also be charged with control over the emergency program budget to ensure its planning direction and initiatives coordinate with fiscal resources.

In addition to ensuring that a Comprehensive Emergency Management Plan is in place, the Committee is responsible for ensuring an active program of hazard analysis, equipment procurement, personnel training and various types of exercises are planned for and executed. In order to achieve these goals, the Committee would be expected to meet frequently enough to monitor the progress of instructions and directions given to the Coordinator. During the normal course of its duties this may be monthly. In initial phases where intense work is occurring on the basic plan, meetings would most likely be more frequent. After that the meetings would be such that they reflected the level of activity directed at the Coordinator.

Also, an annual report should be submitted to Council by the Committee, if not required in the authorizing bylaw or ordinance, summarizing the year's activities and the state of preparedness. The state of preparedness will reflect mitigation efforts as well as those in actual preparedness and recovery planning.

Finally, it is worth noting that the Emergency Program Planning Committee does not have an operational role when an emergency does occur. By definition, its function is in planning to ensure readiness for an emergency. When one occurs those members will be busy in their primary roles as Fire Chief or Police Chief, for example, thus making it impossible, not to mention unnecessary, for the Emergency Program Planning Committee to meet.

ROLE OF THE EMERGENCY PROGRAM COORDINATOR

The role of the Emergency Program Coordinator is unique and one worth exploring. The Coordinator has two roles divided by the planning process and the response role.

In the planning process, the Coordinator works for the Emergency Program Planning Committee facilitating its meetings, either directly or through an elected or appointed chairman, and acts as the technical expert and advisor. The Committee retains overall directional-setting and decision-making power while the Coordinator retains a high level of discretion within that overall direction. It must be a close and efficacious relationship as it is the Coordinator who implements and executes the wishes of the planning committee. The Coordinator conducts or coordinates the research and compilation of supporting information required by the Committee and supervises any outside contractors necessary. The Coordinator is expected to report to the Committee on an ongoing basis, the frequency of which will be determined by importance and scope of the particular task delegated to him/her.

Further, the Coordinator is expected to operate within the budgetary constraints placed by the Committee. The Committee should be granted certain funds by the municipal Council to achieve its mandate. The Committee is responsible for operating within these limits and it is generally the Coordinator who drafts the budget for the Committee's ratification. The Coordinator reports on the progress of the planning initiatives of the Committee and how this is reflected in budgetary expenditures.

The second role of the Emergency Program Coordinator is in the response phase during an emergency. The Coordinator is responsible for executing the emergency plans put in place by the planning committee. When the call is made to implement the plan, i.e., there is a need for a coordinated response to a significant emergency and the important decision makers are needed in one place, it is the Coordinator who will gather the required participants. Once those required have gathered in the Emergency Operations Center, the Coordinator then acts as an expert advisor to this group. It is the municipal Chief Administrative Officer who retains his/her position as the primary non-elected decision-maker by acting as the chair of this "meeting." The Coordinator will ensure that this group of decision-makers has all the information and supplies needed to respond to the emergency. This includes acting as the liaison with other agencies and controlling communications and volunteers. The Coordinator will also handle routine media inquiries and facilitate statements by the Mayor and Chief Administrative Office to the media.

It is worth noting that the role of the Mayor and Council may vary. The Canadian "weak mayor" system usually sees the Mayor and Council deferring routine emergency management to the Chief Administrative Officer but remaining informed and providing guidance where the Mayor or Chief Administrative Officer feel it is appropriate or necessary. In cases where a state of local emergency has been declared the Mayor is the person invested with the extraordinary powers and plays a more prominent role. The American "strong mayor" system sees the Mayor playing a more active role in routine management and can then best decide how, subject to any statutory requirements, to keep his Council informed. Beyond these two systems, the role of the Mayor and Council will vary in other countries.

As the response phase transitions into the recovery phase, the Coordinator shifts emphasis from assisting municipal managers in the Emergency Operations Center with response priorities and resource allocation issues to executing the Service Continuation Plan and other recovery issues.

The essential aspect in differentiating these two roles, planning and response, is for whom the Coordinator works. Whereas in the planning function the Coordinator worked for the planning committee as a resource, the Coordinator changes to being that same technical expert, advisor and facilitator to the municipal Chief Administrative Officer or Mayor when the Emergency Operations Center is set up.

The Coordinator is not intended to be the person who runs the Emergency Operations Center. The Emergency Operations Center is simply a gathering of all the senior municipal managers under the chair of the Chief Administrative Officer with all the resources and communications necessary to manage an extraordinary situation as long as it remains within the capability of the local government. The Coordinator is the advisor to this group but also ensures, on behalf of the Chief Administrative Officer, that the plan has been properly executed (or the necessary parts thereof if it is only a partial activation) so that all resources required by the managers are in place to allow them to make the necessary decisions and to communicate those to the field.

It is at this time that the Coordinator has a great deal to do. Not only is he or she required to be on top of the current emergency situation so that he or she can offer timely and appropriate advice to the managers, but also to act as the "director" to ensure the many facets of executing the plan, calling out the required staff, setting up the Emergency Operations Center, ensuring emergency communications are present and ensuring that the public information function is getting accurate and timely information to the media for dissemination.

In addition to sound experience in emergency planning and management, the role of Emergency Program Coordinator requires tremendous skill at multitasking and delegation as well as tact, good judgement and superb communication skills.

CONCEPT OF OPERATION

Prior to undertaking the *Comprehensive Emergency Management* approach, it is necessary to articulate the basic assumptions, premises, institutional culture, motivation and executive endorsement which are driving the creation of this plan, in addition to the constraints and impediments within and around the organization. It may also touch on the legislated mandate to deliver services where applicable. The *Concept of Operation*[1] is the all-important statement which precedes any planning endeavour and states the mission of the organization doing the planning, what business/service functions are critical to surviving an emergency, how the organization views the continuation of these services taking place and why it is critical to ensure their continued provision.

This statement should be as brief and concise as possible and appear as the preamble to the Comprehensive Emergency Management Plan. As the authoritative statement, the *Concept of Operation* forms the foundation for the planning activities that follow and provides the general guidance on establishing planning priorities.

THE PLANNING PROCESS

"Planning" as a process is a generic one applicable to virtually any aspect of personal or professional thought development and evolution. It provides a logical, normative framework which directs the evolution of a concept to a workable, implementable state and provides for its ongoing maintenance as a means of keeping it focussed, relevant and true to the original purpose.

Emergency planning, therefore, like any other planning endeavour, follows a common process which consists of the following points:

- *identify* the issues;
- *evaluate* the issues;
- *develop* a plan;
- *analyze* the plan;
- *implement* the plan; and,
- *maintain* the plan.

The Emergency Program Coordinator must not lose sight of how the planning process applies in developing a Comprehensive Emergency Management Plan. The principles of the planning process are used to provide a necessary conceptual organization to problems at multiple levels. The process applies in the overall scheme of ensuring that not only is a Comprehensive Emergency Management Plan put in place, but also to subcomponents of the overall goal. As we will see, this process will be called upon to assist the Emergency Program Coordinator through mitigation efforts, developing the Preparedness Plan and ensuring service continuation and other recovery initiatives have not only been fully thought through for efficacy but are subject to annual review to ensure relevance.

The planning process is a simple, common sense framework to keep in mind when tackling any planning effort. It is a concept which the successful Emergency Program Coordinator should embrace and readily employ.

NATURE OF LOCAL GOVERNMENT EMERGENCY PLANS

Local emergency plans are developed in each jurisdiction from basic, fundamental analysis simply because the political environment, organizational culture, community values, potential hazards and the degree of exposure for each are unique to each individual community. A "cookie cutter" approach to emergency planning is not a viable option as no "off-the-shelf plan" can put the proper emphasis on the highest probability hazards faced by a specific community, nor can it attempt to fathom the complex and often paradoxical political and organisational peculiarities of a local government. Therefore, proper emergency planning education calls for imparting on the Emergency Program Coordinator the fundamental analysis and skills necessary to conduct a proper planning effort starting at a very simple and basic level. As we will see, as this elementary analysis is done it will lead to the development of specific components which will eventually aggregate to a Comprehensive Emergency Management Plan for the jurisdiction in question.

The constituent parts that will eventually aggregate to become the Comprehensive Emergency Management Plan must cover an array of areas from ensuring an adequate response to an emergency to providing for displaced persons and ensuring local government service provision continues on an as normal as possible basis. This will be made clearer as subsequent chapters proceed through the full planning process.

SCOPE OF APPLICATION

Once a Comprehensive Emergency Management Plan is developed, the provisions detailed therein may be employed for all types of emergencies ranging from the "routine," such as industrial spills, to catastrophic events, such as a major earthquake. The concept behind such a plan is flexibility. The general provisions and protocols can be invoked for any scale of emergency which requires the local government to adopt a "special operating status." This could be staffing the Emergency Operations Center twenty-four hours per day with just a few staff and technical experts to monitor a chlorine spill at an industrial site, or a full-scale emergency where extensive coordination resources require the local government to make allocation decisions.

Avoid planning only for "the big one" as this mindset generates a plan envisioning such a catastrophic emergency that its provisions do not allow it to be used in smaller emergencies. Such plans are rarely absorbed by an organization, and a plan that is not realistic, applicable, widely available and understood, is of no use.

In the comprehensive planning exercise to be followed in this document, a range of possible relevant hazards will be identified for one's specific region, and a mitigation, preparedness, response and recovery plan will be identified for each. The majority of a Comprehensive Emergency Management Plan will be common standard operating procedures applicable to most eventualities. Confidence in the management structures written in the plan will allow each local government to face these threats and adapt to changing circumstances in an effective and efficient manner.

COMPREHENSIVE EMERGENCY MANAGEMENT

Comprehensive Emergency Management is the concept which ensures that all aspects of anticipating, minimizing the risks from, preparing for and recovering from, an emergency are systematically addressed. The generic planning process previously referenced underscores the most common approach to effectively dealing with emergencies and is embodied in the logic of *Comprehensive Emergency Management* as a concept. *Comprehensive Emergency Management* consists of four phases:

- Mitigation;
- Preparedness;
- Response; and,
- Recovery.

FOUR PHASES OF EMERGENCY PLANNING

These four phases are the cornerstones to a Comprehensive Emergency Management Planning effort. Each phase will be discussed in detail in subsequent chapters. Within each phase, certain types of emergency plans will be created or certain analysis called for. In each of these sub-areas it is the six steps of the generic planning process which will provide the framework for ensuring each subcomponent remains up to date and relevant. In this fashion, the overall purpose of *Comprehensive Emergency Management* is achieved and retained at a relevant and functional level.

MITIGATION

Mitigation involves identifying potential hazards faced by a community and assessing possible impacts. By employing risk management techniques it may be possible to reduce, deflect or altogether avoid possible impact.

PREPAREDNESS

Preparedness is what most people commonly associate with an emergency plan. It is the phase where response agencies prepare through training and equipment procurement for the event of likely emergencies. Hazard-specific preparedness plans will be developed for specific emergencies while managers prepare to exercise critical decision making in a highly compressed environment and timeframe. Inventories of the items possibly needed to be called upon are also compiled.

RESPONSE

Response is the phase where the Preparedness Plan is executed. Trained and exercised staff should automatically deploy knowing just what to do, based on a properly prepared plan. The response aspect is crisis management and will only be as successful as the effort put into the preparedness phase. The response is not the time to be conducting preparedness-type activities such as compiling lists of providers of generators or heavy equipment. This information must be at one's fingertips for immediate reference.

RECOVERY

Recovery is the most prolonged aspect of *Comprehensive Emergency Management*. A critical aspect of recovery is ensuring the continued provision of the services normally provided by local governments. Some residents will be impacted more or less than others and those residents will want service levels restored to as close to normal as possible as soon as is practical. Accounts payable and receivable, for example, will need to continue so careful thought needs to be given to critical business functions. This will be in addition to the coordination of other recovery events such as post-emergency building evaluation and accounting for residents.

Each aspect of *Comprehensive Emergency Management* forms a complete chapter and will be thoroughly reviewed in turn.

INTERAGENCY COOPERATION AND INTEGRATED PLANNING

In some rare circumstances, a Comprehensive Emergency Management Plan may be invoked to deal with a situation which does not involve other agencies or jurisdictions. Often, this is not the case. By its very definition, an emergency represents a significant situation most likely involving other agencies such as the police, fire or ambulance services, or may physically overlap into another jurisdiction. Such situations necessitate the cooperation of the relevant agencies to work together to attain regionally integrated emergency plans.

Coordination in this area by senior levels of government is generally lacking, resulting in little or no direction in many areas. It is not the function of the municipal

Emergency Program Coordinator to unify the numerous plans in a particular geographic region, rather this person has not only the responsibility to ensure that contingencies are made for liaison with these organizations for the purpose of a well-rounded municipal plan, but also to act in a supportive and cooperative manner when approached by another agency for a similar purpose or when regional coordination activities are undertaken. Integrating one's plan into the other emergency plans which exist in a community will minimize the friction when forced to work together.

THE INCIDENT COMMAND SYSTEM AND ITS APPLICATION AT THE LOCAL GOVERNMENT LEVEL

In order to address this coordination issue, most jurisdictions now embrace the *Incident Command System* (ICS). The Incident Command System was developed by the United States National Wildfire Coordinating Group as a means of effectively integrating the multiple agencies and multiple jurisdictions often endemic in combating large wildfires in many parts of the United States. The result, the Incident Command System, has turned out to be a standardized on-scene emergency management system employed in many parts of the world. The Incident Command System concept is concisely described by the British Columbia Inter-Agency Emergency Preparedness Committee (now Council) as "specifically designed to allow its user(s) to adopt an integrated organizational structure equal to the complexity and demands of single or multiple incidents without being hindered by jurisdictional boundaries. Incident Command System is the combination of facilities, equipment, personnel, procedures and communications operating within a common organizational structure, with responsibility for the management of resources to effectively accomplish stated objectives pertinent to the incident.[2]"

The Incident Command System provides for operations that are either single-agency/single-jurisdiction, multiple-agency/single-jurisdiction or multiple-agency/multiple-jurisdiction. Further, the Incident Command System is divided along functional lines so that appropriately skilled staff perform duties for which they are best suited. This sees the major components of the Incident Command System as management, operations, planning and intelligence, logistics, and finance and administration[3]. The two hallmarks of this system, and the aspects that have gained this system favor as the preferred on-scene emergency management system, are its ability to expand and contract rapidly in a logical manner as the scope and scale of an incident dictates, and its use of common organization, terminology and procedures in all components and facets of the structure. These two aspects overcome the historically most identifiable limitations on large-scale response incidents.

The Incident Command System was developed to fight wildfires, which is an environment where most decision-making occurs on the scene. Local government emergency response involves strategic decision-making at an Emergency Operations Center while tactical decision-making occurs at the scene. As the incident expands the on-scene command structure easily and readily can expand in keeping with the principles of the Incident Command System. A more difficult fit in this expansion of response scope is the role of the local government Emergency Operations Center as the incident grows. The initial jurisdiction may be reluctant to relinquish control of its resources or response efforts especially if a state of local emergency has been declared. This appears to be the one limitation of the Incident Command System as it applies to emergency response involving local governments. In British Columbia, local governments would be loathe to relinquish control and therefore in a multiple-jurisdictional situation one would see multiple local governments retaining some form of operational control over the on-scene commander within its boundaries. Only intervention of the Provincial Government may supersede this, who would then take control most likely by declaring a state of emergency itself for the affected area.

Recently, however, in response to several regional-scale emergencies in British Columbia, wildland/urban interface fire specifically, regional districts are taking on emergency planning as a statutory responsibility providing a scale of emergency management equivalent to American counties. This regional ability to coordinate with the various local governments and to declare its own state of local emergency may resolve this problem. Such coordination issues must be thoroughly resolved before any implementation. This is currently being addressed in British Columbia by regional districts and their consultants whereas the American state/county system has already resolved this. Internationally, regional governments may not exist resulting in the coordination being directly between local and national governments.

PUBLIC INFORMATION

Keeping the residents of a community informed about the extent and severity of an emergency is a critical aspect of effective emergency management. It is an aspect which deserves sufficient and proper planning to ensure nothing gets overlooked when an emergency occurs.

Psychologically, humans seem to be better able to cope with adverse circumstances if they have some idea of what is actually happening to them – parochially referred to as the "big picture." Emergencies may affect different segments of the local population differently. Some residents may be directly impacted by damage or injury, others by evacuation, while others only out of concern for friends and family. These people will either want to know what to do, where to go or whom to call to get answers. Humans, understandably, become emotional, obstinate and uncooperative when faced with events beyond their control. The evacuation of people is eased when people know why, where and for potentially how long they may be evacuated. Also, congestion of telephone switches, cellular phone services, and the tying up of operators and volunteers can be greatly ameliorated by ensuring prompt and concise information is released to the media for immediate dissemination.

Providing emergency public information must be a priority of the local government in its planning initiatives. Poor, inaccurate information, or even relevant information released too late, will not serve any positive purpose not only represents a waste of time and resources, but could have adverse effects. Proper and thorough planning of the public information component will allow that aspect to unfold with a minimum of effort and resources which will be extremely scarce when an emergency occurs.

STATE OF LOCAL EMERGENCY

Declaring a state of local emergency is an option generally available in most provinces and states throughout North America, although the delegation of such extraordinary power in other countries may be limited or nonexistent. Doing so is the highest state a local government can attain and is generally the last resort when a situation escalates. Making such a declaration generally invokes special powers which may then allow the local government to adequately and effectively deal with an emergency.

A state of local emergency is not automatically implied when the local government implements its emergency plan. The Comprehensive Emergency Management Plan is the management system called into use when special coordination is required to meet an extraordinary event. When that event attains a state where special powers are required, a state of local emergency may be declared to address the situation.

The Emergency Program Coordinator must thoroughly research the use of this tool as its use and deployment will vary by country and state/province. For example, in the United States, it is the Governor who declares a state of local emergency in affected counties while in smaller nations without an intermediate level of regional government, the national government may be directly involved in declaring a state of emergency.

Declaration of a state of local emergency may be required to occur in a number of ways depending upon the jurisdiction. The British Columbia <u>Emergency Program Act</u> defines a process which is law in that province but is also highly intuitive and may provide a constructive comment on other province or state requirements for this action.

The Mayor may, at any time he or she is satisfied that an emergency exists or is imminent, declare a state of local emergency relating to all or any specific part of the jurisdiction. The declaration of a state of local emergency must identify the nature of the emergency and the part of the jurisdiction in which it exists or is imminent. Such a declaration must be made one of two ways:
- by bylaw or resolution of Council; or,
- by order of the Mayor who must first use best efforts to obtain the consent of other Council members prior to such order being made, but

them must, as soon as practical after making such a declaration, convene a meeting of Council.

Immediately after making a declaration, the Mayor must forward a copy of the declaration to the Attorney General and publish the details of the declaration by a means that will get the contents of the declaration to the residents in the affected area.

A declaration of a state of local emergency generally expires seven days from the time it is made unless:

- earlier cancelled by Council, the Mayor, the Attorney General or the Lieutenant Governor in Council; or,
- an extension is granted for periods not exceeding seven days each.

Having a fixed time limit on such a declaration means that the Emergency Program Coordinator must keep this in the back of one's mind to ensure that emergency management efforts and those special powers utilized under such a declaration to achieve that end are synchronized to be accomplished in that time frame, or that extensions are sought when needed. In addition, an equal degree of rigor is required as a state of local emergency is terminated. Cancellation is done by either the declaration expiring after the fixed life span of such, or is cancelled by Council, the Mayor, the Attorney General or the Lieutenant Governor in Council. Notification must again be delivered to the public while the Emergency Program Coordinator must ensure those exercising the extraordinary powers either at the order of, or on behalf of, Council is aware of its termination and that the "normal rules of operation" apply again.

While declaring a state of local emergency is the most powerful tool in the local government emergency planning toolbox, it brings on an extra degree of statutory encumbrance to which the Emergency Program Coordinator must devote some of his or her all-too-scarce time and attention.

LARGE-SCALE DECLARED EMERGENCIES

It is not rare for what started as a local emergency to escalate into a large-scale, region-wide or state-wide emergency. Often these are natural events where weather phenomena impact large areas. This topic is worthy of at least a brief mention solely for the purpose of reminding the Emergency Program Coordinator of the importance of the local government being as self-sufficient as possible in terms of emergency planning and response. In some cases the region or state may prioritize the deployment of resources and your local government may not get any or all of its requested support. Also, those supplies and resources that may have been commercially available and suitable for addressing an emergency within your jurisdiction now must serve a much larger population and will no doubt become scarce and insufficient to meet the need. On the international level, foreign aid may be required in large-scale emergencies where such deployment may be determined by the donor and/or the national government.

Finally, the mutual aid agreements negotiated between neighbouring jurisdictions may not be able to be honored in a regional emergency. Evacuating citizens to neighboring areas may not be an option as shelters and evacuation centers may already be in use.

Simply stated, the Emergency Program Coordinator cannot lose sight of where one's jurisdiction operates within the overall context of regional, provincial/state and national-level declared emergencies.

KEY POINTS

- Local government is the first line of response
- In some states/provinces it is mandatory to have local emergency plans; if not, it is sound management
- Senior level management must support and know the emergency plan for it to be effective
- Authority to undertake local emergency planning should be entrenched in a bylaw or ordinance
- Role of the Emergency Program Planning Committee is to determine policy, direct the Emergency Program Coordinator, exercise budgetary control over this program, monitor training and exercises, and conduct an annual review
- Dual role of the Emergency Program Coordinator – in the planning role the EPC researches and compiles the plan under direction of the Emergency Program Planning Committee while in the response role the EPC orchestrates set-up and operation of the Emergency Operations Center while providing support to the assembled decision-makers
- The *Concept of Operation* sets out the local government's reasons for undertaking this process and the opportunities and constraints this creates
- The six step planning process provides the conceptual framework for the overall planning effort as well as for sub-components
- The "cookie cutter" approach does not work. Each community is different and requires individual hazard assessment in light of local conditions and priorities
- Four phases of *Comprehensive Emergency Management*: mitigation, preparedness, response and recovery
- Integrated planning – don't plan in isolation. Speak with neighboring local governments, counties and state/province representatives to ensure appropriate support to and from them is possible
- Incident command system is the emerging standard for interagency coordination
- Emergency public information must be informative, accurate and timely
- State of local emergency is the ultimate step in local emergency response. This usually conveys the extraordinary power to address extraordinary circumstances
- Large-scale declared emergencies may mean little or no support to a local government, so be as self-sufficient as possible.

---

[1] Hussong, W.A. 1994. *So You're the Company's New Contingency Planner!* Disaster Recovery Journal. Jan/Feb/Mar.

[2] Inter-Agency Emergency Preparedness Committee. Undated. A Discussion Paper for an Emergency Management System for British Columbia Based on the Incident Command System Principles.

[3] *ibid.*

2

MITIGATION

> *Prior to undertaking preparedness, response and recovery plans, the local government must first develop an understanding of the types of hazards potentially facing the community and assess the likely impacts of each. This involves identifying hazards, identifying the types of impacts that may affect various systems, taking steps to minimize these impacts, communicating these efforts and letting staff and the public know which hazards cannot be addressed.*

LESSENING THE IMPACT

Mitigation is the first of the four phases identified under *Comprehensive Emergency Management*. It is the process by which the impact of potential emergencies may be reduced, deflected or avoided altogether. It is one of the most critical of the four phases of *Comprehensive Emergency Management* as it involves recognizing hazards and coming to terms with the potential impact.

Of greatest importance are the steps that can be taken to protect facilities and service delivery functions from disruption. This action, which in some cases may be costly if, for example, proper hazard assessments were not done prior to the placement of facilities, must be based on a sound understanding of the issue (the hazard) and balanced against the risk of continuing to do business in an exposed setting. This section will outline the steps necessary to mitigate potential emergencies starting with a proper risk assessment to identify hazards and to assess ones vulnerability, managing the risk based on the identified exposure(s), educating those affected by the risk and taking preventative steps to avoid being impacted by the identified hazards.

THE CONCEPT OF RISK

Risk is an important concept that every Emergency Program Coordinator must thoroughly comprehend. While it is important to recognize that no activity can be totally immune from risk as it can never be totally eliminated, it usually can be reduced to an acceptable level. The following statement captures the essential elements in dealing with risk:

- *risk* is the possibility that harm may occur from an identified hazard;
- *risk analysis* is the process of evaluating the frequency and consequence of the hazard;
- *risk control* uses methods of reducing the frequency or consequences of a hazard; and,
- *risk management* is the ongoing process of daily decision-making given the existence of an identified hazard and that all practical and reasonable measures have been taken to minimize any potential impacts it may have[1].

Risk is more simply described as frequency multiplied by consequence. In terms of emergency planning, risk is the frequency of an identified hazard facing a community and the consequences that may result. It is this basic concept the Emergency Program Coordinator should keep in the forefront of one's mind as the hazard analysis exercises in the remainder of this section are reviewed. In some cases, hazards can be readily addressed to a point where either the likelihood of occurrence is minimized or the impacts ameliorated to a level which is tolerable. In some cases hazards are of a nature where, for various reasons, they cannot be addressed and represent an ongoing imminent threat to the local government. This is the nature of risk analysis and management as it applies to the mitigation phase of *Comprehensive Emergency Management.*

OBJECTIVES

Mitigation has four objectives: eliminate the hazard, reduce the risk, reduce the consequences and spread the risk[2].

ELIMINATE HAZARDS

Emergency planners often add new sections to existing emergency plans to enable responders to deal with new threats. A better course of action, depending upon the risk and potential impact, would be to eliminate the hazard altogether. Of course, some hazards such as earthquakes and tornadoes cannot be eliminated; however, hazards such as toxic waste depots could be relocated, and transportation of dangerous goods could be re-routed. It may be far more practical and cost-efficient to eliminate the hazards rather than plan to deal with their impact[3].

Thus, the Emergency Program Coordinator may find one's self in a position of trying to influence local authorities to deny approval for, or to relocate, certain hazardous facilities. It is important to not only consider existing hazards but to also anticipate incurring or attracting further hazards. These will include hazardous activities and sites with their associated by-products.

REDUCE RISKS

Eliminating some hazards may be impossible, but it may be possible to reduce the risk of an emergency occurring. For example, it is usually impossible to move an airport or change a flight path, but it is possible to be aware of existing standards and steps being taken to reduce the risk of an aircraft crash. Where standards are not being followed or are inadequate, the Emergency Program Coordinator should take steps to ensure that the community is aware of the situation and be proactive in lobbying for support and change.

In many cases it is only after an emergency in another community or country that people become concerned about their own community. The important concept for the Emergency Program Coordinator to keep in mind is that of anticipation: anticipate the risk, examine the standards for risk reduction, and determine the adequacy of standards and enforcement of those standards[4].

REDUCE CONSEQUENCES

If a hazard can not be eliminated, and the risks have been reduced to acceptable levels, there are two steps that can be taken in order to reduce the consequences: mitigate the impact, and prepare a response.

For example, if it is impossible to re-route dangerous goods transportation, it may be possible to move critical facilities adjacent to the route. This applies both in an injury reduction sense, in that the siting of institutions next to hazardous facilities or routes must be minimized, and in a physical infrastructure sense by being aware of where roads, rail, pipelines and bulk storage converge. The Emergency Program Coordinator should be aware of both potential emergency sources, such as the storage and use of chlorine gas, and the siting of new health facilities or schools so that infrastructure required in an emergency response does not become part of the problem[5]. Plans to respond to such emergencies are then in order and developed in the preparedness phase of *Comprehensive Emergency Management*.

SPREAD RISKS

"Spreading the risk" is an expression usually associated with the insurance industry. Indeed, it may be time for a local government to work with its insurers to investigate the costs and benefits of retrofitting facilities for earthquakes, flood-proofing and extreme weather, and the effect this would have on the financial stability of the local government before and after an emergency.

Another approach is to play an active role in planning processes. This applies both proactively, to avoid disastrous situations as mentioned, and retroactively, as part of public hearings and investigations after an emergency, especially if it is human-caused, when the combination of circumstances is reviewed and the Emergency Program Coordinator may have input to avoid future emergencies.

Community awareness and education are critical components in hazard mitigation. When possible, this message should be taken to the public. This however, moves emergency planning into the political arena, pushing Emergency Program Coordinators into what, for many, may be an uncomfortable situation. However, for emergency management to be taken seriously, both as a profession and a responsibility, Emergency Program Coordinators must take a more proactive approach[6].

Mitigation Checklist

Objectives
Eliminate Hazards
Reduce Risks
Reduce Consequences
Spread Risks

Risk Assessment
Hazard Identification
    Internal Hazards
    External Hazards
    Hazard Inventory
Vulnerability Analysis
    Impact Assessment
        Types of Impacts
            Social
            Environmental
            Economic
            Political
        Systems Impacted
            Regulatory
            Human
            Building
            Business
    Ethnic and Cultural Consideration

Risk Management
Types of Losses
    Personnel
    Property
    Expenses
    Liability
Five Steps
    Identify Exposures
    Examine Risk Management Techniques
        Risk Control
            Exposure Avoidance
            Loss Prevention
            Loss Reduction
            Segregation of Expenditures
            Contractual Transfer
        Risk Financing
    Select Best Technique(s)
    Implement Selected Technique(s)
    Monitor and Revise Approach

Risk Communication
Education
    Staff
    Public
Prevention

Risk Assessment

A comprehensive risk assessment is fundamental to hazard mitigation and reflects the duality of local government emergency planning. Not only must the hazards be identified that will impact upon the facilities, service delivery and staff of a local government, but the impact on the community in general must also be anticipated in order to assess the potential evacuees and casualties that may be generated through various types of emergency. Hence, there is a need to identify the potential hazards facing the community in general, and a need to assess the vulnerability to these hazards by anticipating the type and extent of the impact.

Hazard Identification

A hazard is considered to be anything which either threatens the residents of a community or the things that they value. In the context of a local government, a hazard is anything which threatens its facilities, service delivery function, staff, or has the potential to generate a large number of evacuees and casualties.

A basic aspect of emergency planning is to complete a thorough hazard assessment. This may allow the elimination or mitigation of existing hazards, thus possibly avoiding the need to develop response plans to deal with them. Based upon this assessment of the hazards facing a community, the remainder of the Comprehensive Emergency Management Plan will specifically identify certain response tactics or retain sufficient flexibility to adapt to a wide variety of hazards.

Internal Hazards

The logical first step in hazard identification is to identify those within the community, jurisdiction or service delivery area. Most hazards fall into three categories: natural hazards, such as earthquakes, forest fires and windstorms; human-caused hazards, such as aircraft crashes, toxic chemical spills and oil spills; and social hazards, such as riots, war and disease.

While these examples represent the full range of potential internal hazards facing a community, the inclusion of some or all of these will eventually depend upon the budget, information and time available. However, an *all hazards* approach is highly recommended at this stage. Do not discount certain considerations simply because they have not happened or the likelihood is extremely rare: emergencies are extraordinary situations brought on by extraordinary circumstances.

Experts in meteorology, fire fighting, engineering and environmental chemistry should be consulted for guidance on the frequency and severity of certain kinds of events. Where a lack of information or historic record presents itself, the Emergency Program Coordinator may have to develop some possible scenarios to fully develop the possible events and necessary reactions.

The more thought put into this step of the planning process, the more flexible, and hence durable, will be the overall plan. This will eliminate any second-guessing of the emergency plan's ability to deal with potentially any hazard when those extraordinary situations arise.

EXTERNAL HAZARDS

It is foolish for an Emergency Program Coordinator to constrain one's analysis, planning and preparedness to a specific jurisdiction without considering the hazards and planning endeavours of adjacent jurisdictions.

This is an important consideration for local governments. Emergencies occurring in a neighboring jurisdiction, even if not affecting this local government directly, may have a significant impact on the local resources if expertise and equipment need to be seconded or evacuees need shelter. Mutual aid agreements, common in the police and fire services, may need to be negotiated between a local government and one or all of its neighbours. If a particular jurisdiction is highly susceptible to large-scale incidents, such as the one which contains the regional airport, it is advisable to coordinate plans for this eventuality.

HAZARD INVENTORY

Most emergency plans include some form of hazard description. The simplest form is a list of hazards that local experience and local experts suggest may occur. This method may be faulty as the less frequently or randomly occurring phenomena may not be represented. In keeping with the concept of an all hazards approach, as comprehensive a list of hazards as possible should be articulated. *Figure 1* presents a sample checklist of hazards which may be considered in your community or jurisdiction.

Figure 1
Inventory of Community Emergency Probability[7]

Rate the probability of the following events occurring in your community over the next decade according to the following scale:

0 - not applicable to my community
1 - not probable
2 - low probability
3 - moderate probability
4 - high probability
5 - nearly certain

0 1 2 3 4 5 AVALANCHE
0 1 2 3 4 5 BLIZZARD OR MASSIVE SNOWSTORM
0 1 2 3 4 5 BOMB THREATS
0 1 2 3 4 5 ACTUAL BOMBING
0 1 2 3 4 5 CHEMICAL CONTAMINATION OR SPILL
0 1 2 3 4 5 CIVIL DISOBEDIENCE OR RIOT
0 1 2 3 4 5 DAM RUPTURE
0 1 2 3 4 5 DROUGHT
0 1 2 3 4 5 EARTHQUAKE
0 1 2 3 4 5 ELECTRIC POWER BLACKOUT
0 1 2 3 4 5 EPIDEMIC
0 1 2 3 4 5 MAJOR STRUCTURE FIRE
0 1 2 3 4 5 FLASH FLOOD
0 1 2 3 4 5 FOREST OR BRUSH FIRE
0 1 2 3 4 5 FREEZING ICE STORM
0 1 2 3 4 5 HOSTAGE INCIDENT
0 1 2 3 4 5 HURRICANE FORCE WINDS LOST PERSONS
0 1 2 3 4 5 MAJOR FROST AND FREEZE
0 1 2 3 4 5 MAJOR GAS MAIN BREAK
0 1 2 3 4 5 MAJOR HAIL STORM
0 1 2 3 4 5 MAJOR INDUSTRIAL ACCIDENT
0 1 2 3 4 5 MAJOR INFRASTRUCTURE FAILURE OR DISRUPTION
0 1 2 3 4 5 MAJOR ROAD ACCIDENT
0 1 2 3 4 5 MAJOR SMOG EPISODE
0 1 2 3 4 5 MAJOR WATER MAIN BREAK
0 1 2 3 4 5 MINE EMERGENCY
0 1 2 3 4 5 MUD OR LANDSLIDE OIL SPILL
0 1 2 3 4 5 PIPELINE EXPLOSION
0 1 2 3 4 5 PLANE CRASH IN THE COMMUNITY
0 1 2 3 4 5 RADIOLOGICAL ACCIDENT
0 1 2 3 4 5 RIVER FLOOD
0 1 2 3 4 5 SEVERE FOG EPISODE
0 1 2 3 4 5 SHIP EMERGENCY IN HARBOUR OR NEARBY COAST
0 1 2 3 4 5 SMALL BOAT LOST OR ACCIDENT
0 1 2 3 4 5 SUDDEN WASTE DISPOSAL PROBLEM
0 1 2 3 4 5 RAILWAY ACCIDENT
0 1 2 3 4 5 TORNADO
0 1 2 3 4 5 TSUNAMI
0 1 2 3 4 5 VOLCANIC ERUPTION OR FALLOUT
0 1 2 3 4 5 WATER POLLUTION
0 1 2 3 4 5   • WATERSHED
0 1 2 3 4 5   • WELL CONTAMINATION
0 1 2 3 4 5   • OTHER GROUND WATER SOURCES
0 1 2 3 4 5   • BACK-UP OF SEWAGE TREATMENT PLANT
0 1 2 3 4 5 WATER SHORTAGE
0 1 2 3 4 5 OTHER (DESCRIBE)

This list is not inclusive of all possible emergencies but is meant to serve as a first step in identifying community threats.

VULNERABILITY ANALYSIS

Vulnerability analysis is an assessment of the impact that given hazards may have, not only on your community, but on your emergency response system as well. Each hazard has a particular type of impact on a community and the response mechanisms. For example, floods limit mobility while windstorms may render communication systems inoperable and chemical spills can produce mass casualties. Not only must a local government be aware of how each hazard will impact their facilities, service delivery and staff, but also the potential for generating casualties from the emergency and the constraints placed on responders due to the nature of the event.

IMPACT ASSESSMENT

Understanding the potential hazards and associated risks in a community is important. To determine the priorities in addressing these hazards, it is important to consider the possible impact of each.

There are four types of impacts: social, environmental, economic and political[8]:

- *Social impacts* are factors such as the numbers of deaths and injuries resulting from a particular hazard. Other social impacts to be considered are the loss of existing housing, disruption of education and the loss of critical facilities and irreplaceable or difficult to replace equipment.
- *Environmental impacts* include the effect of a hazard on air and water quality. The effects on existing wildlife and vegetation also warrant consideration.
- *Economic impacts* would include structural and non-structural damage, loss of infrastructure, loss of transportation centers, and the temporary or long-term loss of jobs.
- *Political impact* is reflected by public perception of blame, or the degree to which local officials are held responsible for the occurrence and response to the emergency. This last point is of particular concern to local governments as protectors of the public health.

In addition to these *types* of impacts, the Emergency Program Coordinator must consider the components, or *systems,* the impacts bear upon and possibly alter. These are: regulatory, human, building and business[9]. The nature of the regulatory environment, either within the local government or from outside bodies, may change in the aftermath of an emergency. This is particularly true in hospital and public health areas where more stringent measures may be necessary in such conditions.

Also, senior levels of government may become involved if a significant event has occurred.

The human environment will certainly have change after such an event. Contrary to popular perception, widespread panic is not common after major emergencies. Rather, the reality will be people in shock and concerned for their families. It may be difficult to have people on the job focus on their duties or to have people report to work if the event occurred while they were at home. In addition, in the case of a significant emergency, the apparently insurmountable job of cleaning up and carrying on with business may affect the performance of administrative staff. Critical Incident Stress Debriefings will most likely be necessary in major emergencies and need to be anticipated.

The physical infrastructure of the work environment may be impacted and necessitate a change of venue. Alternate locations and proper seismic evaluations must be part of a comprehensive plan.

Finally, the business environment will be impacted. In local government, this equates to over-burdened resources. This will involve a crisis management team practiced in this type of management. This activity may also detract from other routine but necessary business functions of the local government.

ETHNIC AND CULTURAL CONSIDERATIONS

Many recent immigrants may have difficulty understanding the commonly spoken language of the community and have trouble understanding orders to evacuate, following emergency procedures and seeking appropriate medical aid. In addition, they may not understand or assimilate hazard information and emergency preparedness material.

Ethnic minorities are often unaware of programs for financial, emotional and medical assistance following an emergency. The inability of minorities to get aid means there is a longer period of economic recovery and that may mean a long-term decline in the quality of life. Those persons with the highest damage report high loss levels, and they receive the most aid, but those with the littlest to lose and, thus, the lowest financial losses are often the most in need.

Given the added risks that are associated with belonging to an ethnic or cultural minority, it is crucial that Emergency Program Coordinators work with ethnic groups in their communities to ensure the adequate provision of basic humanitarian services following an emergency.

RISK MANAGEMENT

Risk management is the corollary of risk assessment. Whereas risk assessment is the identification of hazards and their potential impact on a community, risk management is the weighing of the probabilities of an activity or activities leading to a consequence which has a negative impact on a community. In other words, it is the balance of continuing to do business "as is" versus taking potentially costly and inconvenient steps to mitigate a hazard.

The formally defined purpose of risk management is "to provide a systematic tool for anticipating potential losses to an organization, and for selecting the most effective means of reducing losses[10]." In its broadest sense, risk management deals with four types of losses[11]:

- *Personnel Losses* - loss of the services of key people due to sickness, injury or death. Personnel losses affect the efficiency of your operation, especially where you count on someone who has unique skills or knowledge to help you meet your objectives.
- *Property Losses* - any tangible property, such as equipment, supplies or facilities belonging to an organization that is lost due to accidental events. Property losses may involve theft, physical damage from carelessness or a natural or human-caused emergency.
- *Expenses* - additional costs incurred due to an accident such as supplementary staff, additional supplies or transportation costs. These losses account for extra expenses that would not have arisen without the emergency.
- *Liability Losses* - this category includes the personnel, property or expense losses of others outside the organization due to the alleged wrongful acts of an organization's agents. Any expenses incurred to defend or administer a claim are liability losses.

Therefore, the most commonly articulated objectives of risk management are:
- to ensure personnel safety;
- to reduce losses of supplies and facilities;
- to reduce negligence by staff; and
- to minimize public risk.

These objectives should be kept in mind during mitigation activities, and risk assessment activities in particular. These may help guide what hazards must be mitigated and which can be "risk managed." Once again, the Emergency Program Coordinator must not forget the duality of this function: not only is the protection of facilities, staff and service delivery an important aspect, but also preventing the exposure of the general public to an unacceptable risk is equally important.

Five simple principles of risk management will help make this aspect of mitigation easier to integrate[12]. These are: *be professional, be thorough, be prepared, keep a record* and *talk with people*. Acting in an appropriate and competent manner, being thorough in your task, preparing for questioning and criticism, maintaining accurate records of activities and decisions, and talking with people to share your concern over minimizing exposure to risks will assist in making risk management an effective part of emergency mitigation.

The five steps in risk management are: *identifying exposures; examining risk management techniques; selecting a technique; implementation*; and, *monitoring*[13].

IDENTIFY EXPOSURES

An exposure is a threat, such as the hazards identified in an earlier stage of the planning process. In addition, it can include liability exposure arising from statutory obligations and other Acts such as the Workplace Hazardous Materials Information System (WHMIS). The actions required under this step are largely done in the earlier hazard identification section of risk assessment.

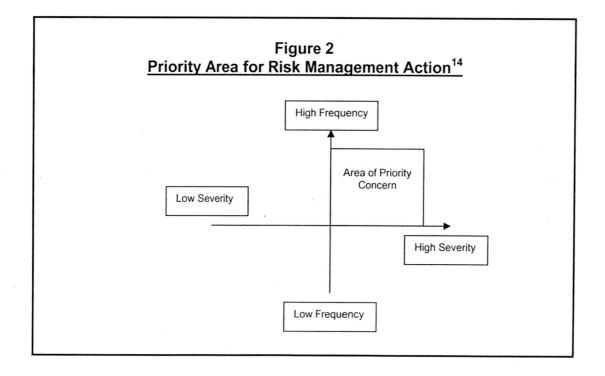

Figure 2
Priority Area for Risk Management Action[14]

Figure 2 shows where the greatest concern should be placed based on the frequency and severity of exposures (hazards).

EXAMINE RISK MANAGEMENT TECHNIQUES

There are two general approaches to manage risk: focus on control measures to minimize potential losses, known as *risk control;* and *risk financing* which accepts the exposure and pays for actual losses after the event by either retention, where the organization assumes financial responsibility, or through commercial insurance. Clearly, risk control is the most responsible option for a local government.

Risk control techniques attempt to reduce the probability and consequences or accidental losses. There are five common risk control techniques: *exposure avoidance, loss prevention, loss reduction, segregation of exposures* and *contractual transfer.*

EXPOSURE AVOIDANCE

The best way to reduce exposure to risk is to stop the risky activity. This would entail stopping certain activities altogether and implies an option for discretionary activities. This is not an option for mandated actions.

From a facility perspective, siting of proposed facilities should be given careful thought to ensure risks to the building and staff are eliminated. From a public health perspective, certain post-emergency epidemiological concerns may be eliminated by taking proactive steps to eliminate certain contributing factors. The objective is to reduce the probability of risk to zero.

LOSS PREVENTION

Loss prevention also attempts to reduce the probability of risk but not as ambitiously as exposure avoidance. Loss prevention focuses on reducing the loss frequency and not the severity. Minimizing the number of times a risky activity is undertaken, or the exposure of facilities, staff or service delivery functions to a risk, will reduce the probability of a loss occurring.

LOSS REDUCTION

Loss reduction focuses on the severity of the impact when loss prevention has failed. This would involve well thought out plans for moving to alternate locations should a facility be impacted by an emergency; the off-site storage of back-up records; or, mutual aid plans for calling on neighboring local governments. Real reduction of the impact depends upon such ameliorating actions taking place almost automatically after an emergency.

SEGREGATION OF EXPOSURES

Segregation of exposures naturally follows from loss reduction with two options: segregate supplies, service delivery function or management operations to a number of locations to minimize the probability of one emergency at one facility from becoming a catastrophe; or duplication of supplies and service delivery capability.

Segregation would imply a certain degree of inefficiency in an organization and travel time and cost, whereas duplication implies an added expense in duplicate material and time in cross-training staff.

CONTRACTUAL TRANSFERS

This technique involves transferring some or all of one's function to a contractor who accepts the risk exposure. Clearly, this is not an option for a local government for the majority of its mandated functions. However, it is something that should be specifically articulated in routine contracts involving some risk exposure such as gas and hazardous chemical delivery and hazardous material disposal.

SELECT BEST TECHNIQUES

Selecting the apparent best risk management alternative means selecting the most workable techniques based on four criteria: technical feasibility, financial constraints, legal requirements, and humanitarian considerations.

- *Technical feasibility* simply involves matching the technical needs of facilities, management or the planning process to the method and outcome of a particular technique.
- *Financial constraints* are perhaps the most significant in their impact on the choice of technique. Implementation and management of the techniques must be financially feasible but consideration must also be given to the long-term financial aspect. Cost-benefits studies may be undertaken to assess both aspects of a chosen technique.
- *Legal criteria* are important to local governments to ensure that all aspects of the mandate are met and that all operations are within statutory parameters.

- Finally, *humanitarian concerns* address the human factor in risk control. The saving of lives is fundamental to risk control, mitigation and emergency planning.

IMPLEMENT THE SELECTED TECHNIQUE(S)

Risk control techniques must be implemented to be effective. There are two dimensions to such implementation: technical and managerial. Technical considerations are the most significant and include input from a wide variety of technical experts, such as architects, engineers, geologists, medical doctors and public health professionals. Management considerations provide for the implementation strategies and foster the cultural change within the organization to enable successful transition.

MONITOR AND REVISE APPROACH

The word "apparent" was used in the section on selecting the "apparent" best alternative technique. This is because one cannot be certain of the choice made unless monitoring of the selected criteria occurs.

Ongoing monitoring to observe the correct fit of the chosen technique and the success of the implementation is important to achieving the goal of successful risk control. It should not be assumed that once implemented, the risk control technique looks after itself. Risk control is dynamic as is the operating environment of the organization. Changes to the program may have to be made which might even include adopting a new control technique. In this way, the risk management program will remain current and relevant to the organization.

RISK COMMUNICATION

Risk assessment and risk management activities must be communicated to staff and the public. Efforts made in education and prevention may ease the subsequent *Comprehensive Emergency Management* tasks of preparedness, response and recovery.

EDUCATION

The Emergency Program Coordinator should now have an understanding that communication of hazards and the education of staff, management and the public are an important element in hazard mitigation. The sharing of information is the least costly and most effective form of emergency mitigation. Such simple actions may help save lives by preparing both local government staff and the public for potential emergencies.

Two main elements emerge under "education" which, again, reflect the duality of the local government's function:

- apprise staff of likely scenarios, the steps taken to mitigate theses hazards and how to survive the eventuality of an emergency; and,
- educate the public about likely hazards and the public health threats in the post-emergency period, including the availability of health care facilities, and what they can do to avoid becoming a victim, such as treating water and having personal/family emergency kits available. Taking the message to those target groups in a proactive fashion will help make the jobs of responding and recovering from an emergency much easier.

PREVENTION

Prevention has been alluded to in earlier sections on mitigation, namely as risk control techniques: exposure avoidance and loss prevention. It is worth briefly reiterating as a principle at the close of a discussion on mitigation.

If a potential emergency can be avoided altogether or the exposure to being impacted by a possible emergency can be reduced, time invested in these activities will be seldom wasted. Any effort at prevention becomes magnified in the chain of events which lead up to an emergency. The lives saved and liability litigation which is avoided may save an organization from possible dire consequences in the future.

The same logic applies to costs of preventative actions. Cost incurred in moving facilities, where possible, or retrofitting buildings and infrastructure will prevent interruption of critical service delivery relied upon in the response and recovery phases during and after an emergency. Also, contributing to moving a hazard or applying pressure to local officials to not locate hazards near critical infrastructure are important elements of prevention.

Risk must be anticipated and existing standards for risk reduction must be examined. The adequacy of these standards and their enforcement must be thoroughly assessed. Where such standards are lacking within the jurisdiction, it behoves the Emergency

Program Coordinator to take corrective action and institute standards. Such standards must be simple, achievable and measurable.

Where possible, the Emergency Program Coordinator should be actively involved in prevention measures. Such activities have proven extremely productive in other areas such as fire services and transportation safety. Prevention activities will make the three remaining phases of *Comprehensive Emergency Management*, preparedness, response and recovery, that much easier if all possible action has been taken to avoid unnecessary risk.

KEY POINTS

Mitigation is the first phase of *Comprehensive Emergency Management*

Mitigation reduces, deflects or avoids the impact of potential emergencies

Mitigation objectives: eliminate the hazard, reduce the risk, reduce the consequences and spread the risk

Risk is the possibility that harm may occur from a hazard and is best considered from a frequency versus severity context

Risk analysis is the process of evaluating the frequency and consequence of a hazard

Risk control uses methods of reducing the frequency or consequence of a hazard

Risk management is the ongoing process of daily decision-making given the existence of an identified hazard and that all practical and reasonable measures have been undertaken to minimize any potential impacts it may have

Risk assessment involves an inventory of internal and external hazards and a vulnerability analysis of the type of impact on various systems

Risk management involves reducing four types of losses through identifying exposures and employing various techniques to control risk or simply employing risk financing

Risk communication is the final element of mitigation as staff and public education and prevention activities provide the most cost-effective results community-wide

[1] Modified from the Major Industrial Accidents Council of Canada Basic Risk Assessment Course 1996, pp. 32-33.

[2] Laughy, L. 1990. A Planner's Handbook for Emergency Preparedness. Vancouver: UBC Center for Human Settlements.

[3] ibid. p. 16.

[4] ibid. p. 16.

[5] ibid. p. 17.

[6] ibid. p. 17.

[7] Modified from B.C. Provincial Emergency Program original source.

[8] Laughy, supra.

[9] Perry, L.G. 1994. Preparing for an Emergency: A Step-by-Step Approach. Disaster Recovery Journal. Oct/Nov/Dec.

[10] British Columbia Ministry of Forests. 1990. S-411 Risk Management.

[11] ibid.

[12] ibid.

[13] ibid.

[14] ibid.

3

PREPAREDNESS

Where the potential impact of a hazard cannot be mitigated, a local government must prepare plans for responding to the inevitable. The scope of Comprehensive Emergency Management Planning is huge. Given the resource constraints of a small community, it may take a great deal of time to assemble such prior to it being complete. This chapter will take a unique approach to assembling an all-inclusive plan which starts with certain priority aspects, allowing them to be put in place first, and then followed by subsequent layers of evolving detail being added as these become complete.

EXPECTING THE UNEXPECTED

The preparedness phase of *Comprehensive Emergency Management* is the activity most people associate with "emergency planning." As we now know, preparedness is just one phase of four which address all aspects of an emergency anticipated by a local government, each of which contribute significantly to a particular aspect of avoiding, preparing for, addressing or recovering from the emergency.

Whereas mitigation addresses aspects of avoiding altogether or minimizing the effects of a particular hazard, and recovery, as we will see, deals with ensuring the continuance of critical services and other aspects of recovery once an emergency has occurred, the preparedness phase is closely linked to the response phase. Preparedness is the opportunity to pre-plan and put in place a number of aspects which will occur almost automatically when an emergency occurs or are initiated by a designated official. It provides procedures, checklists, contact information, locations and possible resources which may be required. When an emergency occurs people tend not to think as clearly under the pressure of an unfolding emergency so the ability to rely on procedures and checklists thought out rationally in advance is beneficial to ensuring critical steps are taken immediately and that nothing gets overlooked.

Preparedness will consume a great amount of time since its express purpose is anticipation. Anticipating the needs of the local government to address and respond to a variety of potential hazards takes time to be all-inclusive. While there are a number of philosophies on the structure of preparedness plans, the one proposed herein allows this large task of preparedness to be attacked in a modular manner, focusing first on the core aspects and then adding increasing levels of detail over time. The remainder of this section will present the many aspects of a Preparedness Plan by discussing each while following the outline of an actual plan. Each element will receive a thorough treatment while conveying a template for those reviewing there own existing plans or creating a plan from scratch.

PREPAREDNESS PLANS AT THE FEDERAL AND PROVINCIAL/STATE LEVEL

Preparedness Plans should exist at any level of government where an identifiable hazard poses a threat to a "community" and either the impact is imminent or the consequences of not being prepared for a rare emergency are too great a risk. At the Federal level in Canada there exist preparedness plans for nuclear exposure and for invoking the war measures. In the United States, where the resources are greater and there are a correspondingly larger variety of threats, there exist a wider variety of national-level preparedness plans for such things as biohazardous exposure and terrorist activities. In British Columbia the main provincial-level preparedness plans are the Earthquake Plan and the Flood Plan. Likewise, California's state-level emergency plans include major wildfires, water supply problems and earthquakes.

Internationally, nations will have different preparedness plans based on a number of threats, such as climate, geopolitical situation and endemic disease. Developed nations may see local or regional governments creating sophisticated comprehensive emergency plans while developing nations may still be focusing on basic plans addressing public health and civil order.

The need for preparedness plans at these high levels is to respond to major emergencies where the extensive resources of the particular level of government would be needed. In such scenarios local governments will most likely rely heavily on the support of senior levels of government to address the impact of such a large-scale emergency in their community, as the scale of response is immediately beyond the scope of the local jurisdiction.

Local governments have a responsibility, indeed, in some jurisdictions a legal duty, to prepare to deal with those emergencies which are within the scope of response expected of a local government of a given size.

THE EMERGENCY SPECTRUM

From a local government perspective, the spectrum of emergencies range from "routine" emergencies handled by the traditional response agencies to those major emergencies which may require the declaration of a state of local emergency. The local government then needs a Preparedness Plan that is capable of being applied to a range of possible scenarios. These scenarios cover the spectrum of emergencies from small fires or accidents where no deployment of the Emergency Operations Center is required, to major flooding or weather-related emergencies which require extensive support and coordination from the Emergency Operations Center. Conversely, scenarios can also include a minor motor vehicle accident where a toxic substance is leaked creating a major emergency necessitating full deployment of the Emergency Operations Center. Local governments must plan to respond to this range of possibilities, and having a range of plans based on the size of the emergency is *not* an efficient or effective way to prepare.

One emergency plan flexible enough to cover any scale of emergency is the most successful manner in which to prepare. Supplementing this generally applicable management framework is a series of detailed plans which address specific issues or hazards.

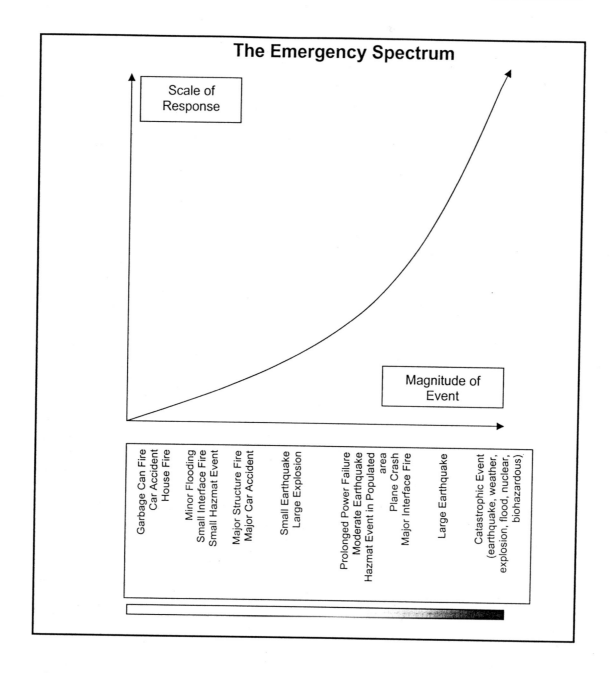

The Emergency Spectrum

Scale of Response

Magnitude of Event

Garbage Can Fire
Car Accident
House Fire

Minor Flooding
Small Interface Fire
Small Hazmat Event

Major Structure Fire
Major Car Accident

Small Earthquake
Large Explosion

Prolonged Power Failure
Moderate Earthquake
Hazmat Event in Populated area
Plane Crash
Major Interface Fire

Large Earthquake

Catastrophic Event
(earthquake, weather, explosion, flood, nuclear, biohazardous)

STRUCTURE OF THE PREPAREDNESS PLAN

Any successful document, plans in particular, must be brief and concisely worded if busy managers are expected to read it and retain the message it conveys. This is particularly true for emergency plans. Some Preparedness Plans are massive documents which attempt to include everything preparedness-related into one document. This only serves to intimidate the reader and results in a document that will rarely be referenced, let alone has any of the information been retained by those essential staff members who need to do so. In observing this fact, it does not mean to imply that these documents include lots of extraneous information. While some may, the majority of preparedness plans are simply constructed in a less than adequate fashion resulting in an intimidating tome when finished but representing a lengthy and costly process from the start of writing until completion. Maintenance and updating of these huge documents can be intimidating, and it is easy to let these critical tasks slip.

In assessing such a task, many local governments unnecessarily contract out this work thinking they have neither the staff time nor resources to do the job. By properly structuring the Preparedness Plan and tackling its many aspects in a prioritized fashion, any size local government can construct a thorough and detailed Preparedness Plan. This structure includes a general Emergency Management Plan as the core, four priority sub-plans covering Emergency Social Services, Evacuation, Telecommunications and Emergency Public Information, and finally hazard-specific preparedness plans for each hazard threatening the local government. While these should all be bound into one binder for convenience, the Emergency Management Plan is employed in every emergency while each of the others addresses a specific aspect which may be employed or for responding to a specific type of emergency.

At the heart of the preparedness effort is the Emergency Management Plan. The Emergency Management Plan is the general, high level document which conveys how all emergencies will be managed. This should be the first plan completed under the preparedness section followed by the four priority plans (emergency social services, evacuation, telecommunications, public information) with the hazard-specific plans to follow in priority order. To that extent, the Emergency Management Plan conveys the management structure which will be employed by the local government to address any emergency that occurs. The essential aspect to this plan is flexibility and incorporates all the general aspects which are common to every emergency. That is not to say that it includes all the detail for each emergency, on the contrary, it ignores hazard-specific detail and concentrates on what is necessary in managing each emergency.

The Emergency Management Plan is the center of preparedness efforts. It is brief and concise in setting out the authority to undertake this plan, in its scope of application, articulating the activation procedure, how the Emergency Operations Center will function and the procedure for declaring a state of local emergency.

The intent of this plan is simply to summarize the authority to act, state the commitment to keeping the public informed, how the Emergency Operations Center gets called into action and who needs to be there, and some general operational guidelines for the Emergency Operations Center such as location and alternate location, equipment, shift rotation, etc. With this, the important decision-makers are in one room with the authority and materials to act, regardless of what the emergency is. It has pulled these players together and has provided for their sustained operation. In that Emergency Operations Center each member continues in his or her normal role in what really amounts to an executive meeting chaired by the Chief Administrative Officer. As a particular emergency unfolds this group works to formulate the best response and control the resources at their disposal to ensure this occurs.

Once an Emergency Management Plan is drafted, and before the detailed planning for each specific hazard, four other areas need to be addressed which are common to, and applicable to, any size of emergency. These are:

- Emergency Social Services Plan;
- Evacuation Plan;
- Emergency Telecommunications Plan; and,
- Emergency Public Information Plan.

These are general in their applicability so as to justify their treatment at this point in the process, yet are specific in their inherent detail to justify each being a separate plan.

These plans can be compiled concurrently as they are sufficiently diverse that each specific sub-committee of the Emergency Program Planning Committee can have unique membership. These plans will address the next critical step once the Emergency Operations Center and its management approach are established, namely how to address the human needs of residents affected by an emergency, how to move residents if necessary, how to communicate under adverse conditions and how to keep the public informed. Once these are in place, the planning committee can focus its attention on the details of specific hazards.

Assuming the Emergency Operations Center is up and operating with all the essential decision-makers present, if it is an emergency that has occurred for which the local government has not anticipated and not created a hazard-specific preparedness plan for, then the Emergency Operations Center will simply have to do its best responding as it sees fit at the time. However, if it is one of the potential hazards identified in the mitigation exercise, the Emergency Operations Center will have the benefit of a hazard-specific preparedness plan to consult.

This is the next step in the preparedness process. Research in the mitigation phase identified the threats facing the local government. These should be prioritized to determine an order, based on either probability or severity, in which they will be tackled. Each hazard-specific preparedness plan should provide a realistic assessment of the threat, what the scale of impact could be, what specific response steps need to be taken, any special duties of certain key people and, finally, lists of resources to be possibly called upon in a catastrophic scenario.

Hazard-specific preparedness plans, of which there most likely will be several for most local government, are plans unto themselves yet should be listed as appendices to the Emergency Management Plan. Doing so will ensure that one binder contains not only that core, flexible Emergency Management Plan, but also all the specific details in these other plans for a wider range of potential emergencies. The subcommittees struck by the Emergency Program Planning Committee will have put great effort into crafting a plan for a specific hazard and attempted to anticipate all facets and needs of such an emergency. That effort should be a considerable aid in responding to that emergency when it actually occurs due to the benefit of pressure-free rational thought put into a response strategy by a group of knowledgeable experts. This certainly cannot be replicated in the Emergency Operations Center as an emergency unfolds so the ability to pull out an appendix of the Emergency Management Plan which deals with this emergency and to immediately get to work is the preferred choice.

In summary, the Emergency Management Plan should be the first plan attempted as it puts in place the system to respond to any emergency. Next should come the four critical aspects of potentially any emergency: the Emergency Social Services Plan, Evacuation Plan, Telecommunications Plan and Emergency Public Information Plan. These are also common aspects of most large emergencies and require more detail on specific subjects than should be in the Emergency Management Plan, therefore, are manifested as separate plans. Finally, come the hazard-specific preparedness plans in order of planning priority. At this stage the Emergency Program Planning Committee can proceed one of two ways: attempt to put in place plans for all hazards identified by concurrently creating rough cursory plans, but have a plan nonetheless; or, to methodically and thoroughly plan for each hazard in turn. Local factors influencing the Emergency Program Planning Committee, or perhaps several hazards of equal potential, may determine the former option as a preference as opposed to a clear list of prioritized hazards allowing them to be addressed completely in turn.

The following illustration shows the structure of what could generally be called the Preparedness Plan. Included are examples of hazard-specific preparedness plans.

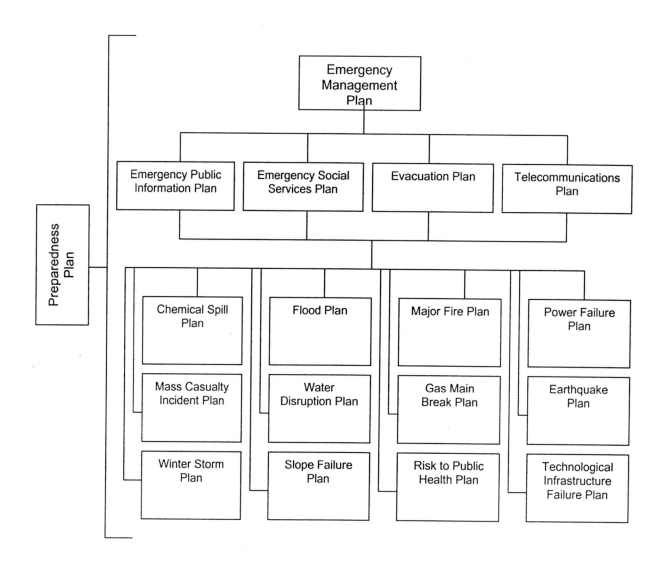

EMERGENCY MANAGEMENT PLAN

The following sections will detail the contents of the Emergency Management Plan portion of the overall Preparedness Plan.

TABLE OF CONTENTS

A table of contents is a simple way of conveying the organization of a document. It is recommended that an Emergency Management Plan have a table of contents simply for quick reference. In keeping with the theme that the Emergency Management Plan is to be a simple and concise document, the table of contents should reflect this by only noting the main headings of major sections and not the detail of sub-headings.

DISTRIBUTION LIST

A distribution list allows the Emergency Program Coordinator to track who has been issued copies of the plan. Further, it also allows those issued with plans to know who else has plans. For the Coordinator, knowing who has copies of the plan allows for easy dissemination of updates when minor changes are made to the plan. When changes are made to the plan a covering memo is sent to those on the distribution list with instructions to replace specific pages in their plans with the attached new pages. When a major re-write of the plan is undertaken, the distribution list shows where to find all copies of the plan to be recalled. This prevents out-dated copies from remaining in circulation which may cause inappropriate outdated actions to be taken in the event of an emergency.

To assist in clarifying which version of the Emergency Management Plan is current, the date of the current version should be noted on the cover page in addition to the date of any plans this version supersedes. Further, this date of the current version should be in the footer or header of each page so as individual pages are replaced with updates, the most current date will show on each page. The Emergency Program Coordinator should maintain the original, or master copy, for control reasons and as a reference if someone has not kept up with their updates. The replacement of certain pages with updates to the plan is made easier if the plans issued to those on the distribution list are in three ring binders.

MAYOR'S ENDORSEMENT

A brief statement from the Mayor should be included at the beginning of the Emergency Management Plan. The Chair of the Emergency Program Planning Committee should invite the Mayor to compose a brief message which conveys the support of the Council for this endeavor, the significance of the plan to the local government and the importance of maintaining it as a relevant and workable document. It sets the tone for the reader/user of the plan that this document has the support of the highest levels and that the procedures and processes detailed therein are relied upon to see the local government through any emergency.

AUTHORITY

The authority which gives the local government the power to make and enforce an emergency plan should be cited. This generally will be a provincial or state statute empowering or, indeed, requiring, local governments to make such plans. This should then be followed by a reference to the local enactment which translates the provincial/state statute into the action at the local level. This would be the local government bylaw or ordinance which is usually designed to prove conformity with the requirement and then establish the programs, committees and positions to achieve the stated goals and objectives.

SCOPE

A brief a statement about the scope of the Emergency Management Plan should be included. This is the opportunity to convey what the plan is intended to address and when it should be called into use. In general, it should note that the plan provides the flexible emergency management framework that is applicable in any type of emergency and usable at any scale of event. It should try to convey the generous applicability of this plan and to dispel the notion that it is to be reserved only for "the big one."

AUTHORIZATION

Although the Emergency Management Plan is applicable to a wide range of emergencies and at almost any scale, it cannot be invoked carelessly. Therefore, authorization for its deployment must be well defined. Exactly by whom and how the plan will be called into action will vary with each local government, yet it must be stated clearly in the plan who may authorize its use and how it will be initiated.

Such control should rest within the senior levels of the local government. In some jurisdictions it may be the exclusive purview of the elected officials, with either the Mayor or at least a Councillor giving the approval. In other jurisdictions senior staff members may be delegated this power. Regardless, clarity is the issue so that the plan is not needlessly abused with resources wasted and costs incurred nor is it left in a state of uncertainty who has the ability to do so.

LINE OF SUCCESSION

The Emergency Program Coordinator is the central figure when invoking the Emergency Management Plan and gathering the required decision-makers in the Emergency Operations Center once authorization is granted. The Emergency Program Coordinator's absence should not hamper this process. While a substitute should be appointed when the Coordinator is not available, e.g., due to holidays, a list of alternates, or line of succession, should be identified. This, then, identifies those capable of acting in the absence of the Coordinator or if he or she is unavailable for whatever reason. For example, such a line of succession after the Emergency Program Coordinator could be the Deputy Emergency Program Coordinator then the Chief Administrative Officer.

ACTIVATION

A clear idea of how activation of the Plan will occur should be articulated in the Plan so those response agencies know whom to contact when an emergency exceeds the scope of their normal capability. Preferably the Coordinator or his or her Deputy will be the first contacted so that a judgement as to the need to invoke the Plan can first be made, since these are the staff best trained to make that decision. The Coordinator will then advise the appropriate person with authority to invoke the plan if they themselves do not have that power. The decision to invoke the Plan is made by the appropriate official, after which the Coordinator begins to gather those required at the Emergency Operations Center. This is usually done via a telephone call-out. The Coordinator is responsible for ensuring that those officials or their alternates are in the Emergency Operations Center as needed, depending on whether the center is fully or partially deployed.

ROLE OF THE EMERGENCY OPERATIONS CENTER

For clarity, it is worthwhile noting the significance of the Emergency Operations Center at this early stage in the Plan. The Emergency Operations Center will serve as the control point for any emergency occurring within the local government's jurisdiction. It is where the decision-makers gather when the Emergency Management Plan is invoked, and becomes the focal point for inquiries from the public and the media. It will be equipped with the necessary supplies to support those decision-makers in responding to an emergency and communicating decisions and requests to and from the field. Its primary function is to support the needs of those responders in the field.

While this may seem like stating the obvious to those initiated in emergency management, it may well be useful information to those users of this plan to whom emergency management is not a day-to-day responsibility.

HAZARD ANALYSIS

Acknowledging the idea of hazard analysis in the Plan is intended to inspire confidence in the user of the Plan that an exercise of anticipating and preparing for a variety of potential emergencies has been undertaken. It should make reference to the appendix in which hazard-specific preparedness plans are found and that these completed plans will be added if missing as the particular planning sub-committee develops that plan. These plans will be completed in order of priority set by the Emergency Program Planning Committee. This will convey the fact that although this Emergency Management Plan may be worded intentionally very generally, it is part of an overall Comprehensive Emergency Management Plan.

PUBLIC INFORMATION

Keeping the public informed about the extent of any "non-routine emergency" is vitally important. Referencing public information at this point of the plan states a commitment by the local government to keeping its citizens informed. As with stating the role of the Emergency Operations Center, this reminds the user of the Plan that public information is a cornerstone of successfully overcoming an emergency and should be an integral part of both preparedness and recovery efforts. Reference should be made to the appendix which contains the detailed Emergency Public Information Plan.

ANNUAL REVIEW

This section is intended to commit to an annual review of the Emergency Management Plan in order to ensure that it maintains relevance and thoroughness. Again, this serves to remind its users that the Plan is not static and that it will be thoughtfully reviewed annually in order to keep up with the dynamic organization it serves and the changing world in which it operates.

This section may go on to further discuss a program of exercises. While the actual timing and conduct of different types of exercises depends on many outside influencing factors, such as the nature of the last actual emergency, the time of the year, and the availability of key participants, it may simply note a commitment to different types of exercises in a general timeframe or be more prescriptive in calling for a specific schedule of exercises (generally achievable due to the annual review).

EMERGENCY OPERATIONS CENTER

The Emergency Operations Center is the control point for every emergency within the jurisdiction of the local government. Because of its importance, the provision for the Emergency Operations Center and the necessary supporting information should be detailed in the Emergency Management Plan. Therefore, the Emergency Operations Center deserves a thorough treatment at this point in the Plan as the first substantive manifestation of preparedness now that the general introductory sections have been addressed.

PURPOSE

Stated concisely, the Emergency Operations Center is the command center for any emergency occurring within the jurisdiction of the local government.

LOCATION

If the local government does not have a room or facility permanently devoted to acting as the Emergency Operations Center, the location of the center must be clearly stated. An Emergency Operations Center can be set up in any large room with sufficient capacity for the required number of people. The center will not have observers or any non-essential persons in the room so capacity only needs to accommodate those designated members with room for modest expansion as necessary. In addition, the room must provide both privacy and security so as not to be on display for the media or unnecessarily interrupted. In choosing an Emergency Operations Center, usually some modification is required if it is not a permanently dedicated facility. Additional phone and fax lines usually need to be added, the availability of uninterrupted power, the ability to monitor the media via cable television, suitable conference and map tables, and comfort amenities such as the availability of washrooms, rest areas, food and beverages, and showers if practical.

An alternate location for the Emergency Operations Center must also be designated. This will be called into use if the primary Emergency Operations Center is rendered inoperable or uninhabitable. Therefore, when choosing an alternate Emergency Operations Center location, one must consider its location when compared to potential hazards which may affect the primary location in addition to the suitability of the room. The location of the alternate site must also be clearly stated in the Plan. The alternate site may not be as completely or thoroughly complimented with the amenities of the primary location but it must be able to meet the basic requirement of being an appropriately sized, safe and secure meeting facility which will permit the decision-makers to consider their response and to communicate this to the field.

A note about Emergency Operations Centers: Emergency Operations Center layout, design and operation is a subject which justifies a book unto itself. Every local government will have either specific needs to accommodate or a unique arrangement which suites their needs. There is no one proper solution to setting up an Emergency Operations Center, and local governments are encouraged during their exercises to experiment with different setups. The recommendations stated here pertain to the overall concept of the Emergency Operations Center, so some of the people and equipment discussed may be located in different rooms within a multi-room center. A communications room is often designated in the Emergency Operations Centers of large local governments to focus all telecommunications in one place. Conversely, in small local governments the Emergency Operations Center may be the Council chamber where everyone gathers. These two examples are at opposite ends of the spectrum and represent different dynamics: the Emergency Operations Center of a large local government will have many people involved and needs segregation to function properly, whereas the Emergency Operations Center of a small local government may have just five to ten people involved who can easily operate in one room.

STAFFING

Those required to be located within the Emergency Operations Center should be identified by title to accommodate the turnover of staff in those positions. The principle of Emergency Operations Center membership is that those who can contribute in a constructive manner to the response phase of an emergency should be there. In addition, the number of people in the Emergency Operations Center should be kept to the very minimum necessary. Each member brings particular expertise in a certain area but also contributes to the synergy of the group by participating in consensus-based decision-making and providing an independent second opinion where and when needed.

In any local government, regardless of size, the Emergency Operations Center should include the following:

- Chief Administrative Officer;
- Emergency Program Coordinator;
- Fire Chief;
- Police Chief;
- Health Official (Medical Health Officer, Hospital Administrator or Ambulance Head);
- Municipal Engineer or Public Works Superintendent;
- Telecommunications Officer;
- ESS Director;
- Public Information Officer;
- Recording Clerk; and,
- Runners, Communicators, Assistants as needed.

These members will be listed with their personal contact information in an appendix for quick reference when the Emergency Operations Center is to be deployed. Alternates for each position should be identified and their contact information be listed in the appendix also. Some positions may require formal delegation to a subordinate when the top official is absent, e.g. Emergency Program Coordinator, Fire and Police Chiefs. Where no formal delegation is practiced, secondary and tertiary alternates need to be identified and accurate contact information maintained in the appendix. Depending on the nature of the emergency, additional participants may be invited to sit in the Emergency Operations Center, such as representatives of the various public and private utility companies.

The Emergency Operations Center is the operations center and as such should not be where the Mayor or Councillors sit. They may tour the facility or observe, but should not play a role in the response coordination. The Chief Administrative Officer, as "chair" of the Emergency Operations Center, is responsible for updating Council and seeking their direction where and when needed. This interaction with Council should take place in a separate room. The Emergency Operations Center then remains as the realm of the response agencies who are skilled at providing the best and quickest response without being encumbered by political debate or those less skilled in emergency response.

During some limited-response emergencies, not all participants listed will be required. In such cases the Emergency Program Coordinator will determine who is required based on the nature and extent of the emergency and contact those persons. Generally, however, if the Emergency Operations Center is being activated most participants will be required.

PROLONGED OPERATIONS

Emergencies requiring the establishment of the Emergency Operations Center will most likely turn into prolonged events requiring relief staff. It is the responsibility of each service or organization participating in the Emergency Operations Center to have identified relief staff to work shifts in the event the center needs to be staffed for prolonged periods. Each service or organization should be prepared in advance with sufficient relief staff to operate the Emergency Operations Center for twenty-four hours per day as would be necessary in the case of a major emergency. The Emergency Program Coordinator should advise those services or organizations of this eventuality and assist them if necessary in such preparations. The Coordinator will also need to work with those Emergency Operations Center staff for which he or she is responsible for arranging relief, e.g. Telecommunications Officer, Public Information Officer, Recording Clerk.

The nature and length of Emergency Operations Center operations varies depending upon the scale and severity of the emergency. Assuming a large-scale emergency which necessitates the full deployment of the Emergency Operations Center, it may operate around the clock for as many days as required until the urgency of the situation has been addressed. At some point operations will begin to wind down, usually following the schedule of work at the site of the emergency (with some exceptions such as flood). When monitoring of a situation, actual response activities, or the caring for evacuees is either completed or becomes a "business hours" operation, the Emergency Operations Center can then be staffed during these hours rather than around the clock.

Eventually the Emergency Operations Center will no longer serve its purpose of supporting actions in the field or monitoring a particular threat. At this point the center may be shut down. It should be noted that shutdown of the center would be dictated by circumstances particular to the local government involved and the nature of the emergency. The Emergency Program Coordinator is best suited to assist in making such a determination.

EQUIPMENT

The Emergency Operations Center will need certain equipment and supplies to function properly. The actual equipment list will vary depending on the size of the local government, the number of staff in the center, whether the center is a dedicated or temporary facility, the concept for how it will be set up and how communications will be addressed, and the preferences of the participants as determined at various exercises.

While it would be impossible to be prescriptive and exhaustive in listing possible Emergency Operations Center equipment and supplies, the types of items to be considered would include:

- conference table with sufficient seating (may consider short standing conferences);
- work stations for each agency;
- map table(s);
- various scale maps of the jurisdiction;
- telephones/radios for each service;
- two fax machines (one dedicated for incoming calls only);
- flip charts;
- white board (for main event log); and,
- stationery supplies (pens, felt pens, paper, thumbtacks, etc.)

A dedicated Emergency Operations Center can slowly evolve to be a well-equipped facility as successive exercises identify possible additions. In such a facility everything will have a place to be stored or installed. In facilities or conference rooms which will be seconded as Emergency Operations Centers, the Emergency Program Coordinator may have a more difficult job of preparing the facility, e.g., telephone jacks, uninterrupted power supplies, radio power, antenna connections, and securely storing supplies. Where a particular service or agency has specific requests that cannot be fulfilled by the local government, that agency will have to supply the equipment in question.

LIABILITY ISSUES

Because extraordinary measures may need to be taken by the local government in the event of an emergency, it may be exposed to certain liability challenges. Conversely, the local government may be challenged for not taking certain actions. Good record keeping during an emergency will be useful in order to verify why certain actions were or were not, taken. Thus, the position of Recording Clerk is an important aspect of the Emergency Operations Center. The Recording Clerk must note all major decisions taken by the Emergency Operations Center collectively and any important circumstances around those decisions. In addition to the notes of the Recording Clerk, each service or organization present in the center must take notes of the decisions made by that agency. Such notes taken during an emergency form a complete record of the local government's response to the emergency. It is the duty of the Emergency Program Coordinator to collect those logbooks and documents and to preserve them in the case legal action is brought against the local government.

This aspect of emergency response is often overlooked but can potentially save the local government from a costly settlement if it is not capable of mounting an effective defence.

STATE OF LOCAL EMERGENCY

Declaring a state of local emergency is the biggest weapon in the local government's arsenal when responding to a major emergency. Because of the significance of this tool it must not only be recognized as such but the powers and procedural requirements of its use should be clearly stated. Most jurisdictions in North America have some ability to either declare a state of local emergency or to have the state or province declare a state of emergency in a specific area. With so many state, province and territorial legislatures enacting some statute to this effect, the procedures to do so and the powers it bestows will vary. The Emergency Program Coordinator must thoroughly research this area and summarize it in the Emergency Management Plan.

For clarity, it is worthwhile noting in the Emergency Management Plan that implementation of the Plan and its deployment of the Emergency Operations Center do not automatically imply the declaration of a state of local emergency. Making such a declaration is an extraordinary event and involves a fixed procedure. Normal use of the Emergency Management Plan and the Emergency Operations Center is the first and usual means of responding to an emergency. It is only when those extraordinary powers which the state of local emergency bestows are required is such declared.

DECLARATION OF STATE OF LOCAL EMERGENCY

Usually there is a clearly articulated procedure for declaring a state of local emergency set out in the enabling statute. It should provide for at least two options for such a declaration to meet most circumstances. For example, the British Columbia Emergency Program Act permits either:

- by bylaw or resolution of Council; or,
- by order of the Mayor who must first use best efforts to obtain the consent of other Council members prior to such order being made, but then must, as soon as practical after making such a declaration, convene a meeting of Council[1].

The Act permits a declaration to be made relating to all or any specific portion of the jurisdiction and such declaration must identify the nature of the emergency.

Enabling statutes should address two other aspects of making such a declaration: public notification and length of the state of local emergency. In British Columbia, for example, it is required that the local government publish the details of the declaration by a means that will get the contents of the declaration to the residents in the affected area. Further, an automatic expiration time is placed on the state of local emergency (7 days in B.C.) if it is not cancelled prior to this date or an extension is granted under other sections. Automatic expiration dates work well as it gives a defined period to address the emergency and requires conscious thought on the part of the Emergency Program Coordinator to monitor this timeframe.

POWERS OF COUNCIL DURING A STATE OF LOCAL EMERGENCY

Declaring a state of local emergency is a serious step and is closely governed by a statute of a senior government, usually a Province or State. The reason for such a declaration is to empower the local government with those extraordinary powers to deal with the emergency, which are not normally part of the local government purview.

In permitting a declaration to be made, the enabling statute generally articulates what that declaration entails in the way of extra powers. These powers should be reiterated in the Emergency Management Plan. This allows for such knowledge to be shared among plan users who then become aware of the full extent of the making of a declaration. Using the British Columbia Emergency Program Act as a guide, these extraordinary powers are of the following nature:

- acquire or use any land or personal property considered necessary to prevent, respond to or alleviate the effects of an emergency;

- authorize or require any person to render assistance of a type that the person is qualified to provide or that otherwise is or may be required to prevent, respond to or alleviate an emergency;

- control or prohibit travel to or from any area;

- provide for the restoration of essential facilities and the distribution of essential supplies and provide, maintain and coordinate emergency medical, welfare and other essential services;

- cause the evacuation of persons and the removal of livestock, animals and personal property from an area of the community that is or may be affected by the emergency; and, make arrangements for the adequate care and protection of those persons, livestock, animals and personal property;

- authorize the entry into any building or on any land, without warrant, by any person in the course of implementing an emergency plan or program or if otherwise considered by Council to be necessary to prevent, respond to or alleviate the effects of an emergency;

- cause the demolition or removal of any trees, structures or crops if the demolition or removal is considered by Council to be necessary or appropriate in order to prevent, respond to or alleviate the effects of an emergency;

- construct works considered by Council to be necessary or appropriate to prevent, respond to or alleviate the effects of an emergency; and

- procure, fix prices for or ration food, clothing, fuel, equipment, medical supplies or other essential supplies and the use of any property, services, resources or equipment within the community for the duration of the state of local emergency.

In addition, the statute should speak to the ability of a local government to appropriate or borrow funds to pay expenses caused by the emergency. This is tightly controlled by the supervising province or state body since this usually implies the necessity to circumvent the public approval or debate component of borrowing or budgeting public funds. Nonetheless, if it is permitted in the statute, it is significant enough to justify specific mention here in the Plan.

CANCELLATION OF A STATE OF LOCAL EMERGENCY

The particular statute will also identify criteria for cancelling a state of local emergency. Generally, a cancellation is worded more or less to the effect that the Council or Mayor must, when of the opinion that an emergency no longer exists in the part of the jurisdiction in relation to which a declaration of a state of local emergency was made, cancel the declaration of a state of local emergency. In keeping with the manner in which a declaration of state of local emergency was made, cancellation of such has two options, either by bylaw or resolution if the cancellation is effected by Council or by order if the cancellation is effected by the Mayor.

Again, as with declaring such, cancellation of a state of local emergency should involve public notification. Cancellation should include immediate notification of the province/state level authority supervising emergency management and the publication of the cancellation which will expeditiously get the message to residents of the area to which the declaration applied.

APPENDICES

The appendices of the Emergency Management Plan contain the detail regarding most aspects of response (except the Emergency Operations Center – the one aspect specifically covered in the Emergency Management Plan). The appendices include duties and checklists for those Emergency Operations Center participants, the emergency telephone callout list, other plans addressing important elements of any emergency such as emergency public information, emergency social services, evacuation and telecommunications, hazard-specific preparedness plans, and miscellaneous but important aspects of emergency response which may be called upon such as:
- Declaration of a State of Local Emergency;
- Evacuation Order;
- Notification of Evacuation Order;
- Mutual Aid Agreements; and,
- Community Resource Inventory.

RESPONSIBILITIES DURING AND AFTER AN EMERGENCY

Each member of the Emergency Operations Center should have his or her responsibilities during and after an emergency articulated along with, or perhaps structured as, an immediate action checklist. This serves two purposes:
- it enumerates the responsibilities of each Emergency Operations Center member and conveys those to each member; and,
- provides a checklist of actions to undertake immediately upon an emergency occurring and the Emergency Operations Center being deployed.

Often, in the minutes following the occurrence of a major emergency, individuals seldom retain the rational thought and presence of mind to institute the necessary steps which should be taken. The most common result is that critical actions simply are overlooked or forgotten. Providing a checklist and consulting it immediately will ensure critically important steps are not overlooked. Each individual local government needs to define these duties and actions, since the multiple variables unique to each jurisdiction are too great to be detailed here.

EMERGENCY TELEPHONE CALLOUT LIST

An accurate and up-to-date list of all those required in the Emergency Operations Center and their designated alternate(s) must be maintained for the plan to be effective. This simply is a listing of the name of the individual and his or her telephone number and alternate contact methods. It should be kept as an appendix for ease of updating allowing individual pages or the entire appendix to be replaced as necessary. This is the list which the Emergency Program Coordinator will consult to notify those required to attend should the Emergency Operations Center be deployed. The Emergency Program Coordinator may call these individuals personally if there are just a few or may develop a telephone fan out with each person being responsible for telephoning just a few other members. This is the most basic communications aspect of the Emergency Management Plan and is fundamental to its success.

EMERGENCY PUBLIC INFORMATION, EMERGENCY SOCIAL SERVICES, EVACUATION AND EMERGENCY TELECOMMUNICATIONS PLANS

These documents are plans unto themselves which detail how certain critical functions will occur during an emergency. These plans are sub-components of the overall Emergency Management Plan and, therefore, appear as appendices to that document,. However, they are plans in their own right detailing specific actions to be called upon when required during a particular emergency. The detail in these plans is too great for inclusion in the main body of the Emergency Management Plan, although the subject must be addressed in the plan. A brief reference in the main body serves to direct the reader to the detail set forth in an appendix. The detailed contents of each of these plans will be outlined later in this section.

HAZARD-SPECIFIC PREPAREDNESS PLANS

The intention of the Emergency Management Plan is to provide the management framework and decision-making structure which will be applied in each major emergency. As we have seen, that cannot include detail on emergency public information, emergency social services, evacuation and telecommunications without becoming a very large, cumbersome, redundant and probably unread document. However, these topics need to be thoroughly addressed as detailed appendices to the Emergency Management Plan.

The same reasoning applies to hazard-specific preparedness plans. The main body of the Emergency Management Plan would be diverted from its primary purpose if it attempted to address all or most of the hazards facing a local government. The prioritized list of hazards facing a community needs thorough analysis and preparation in their anticipation. This work for each of the identified hazards forms a hazard-specific response plan containing a detailed course of action should this emergency occur. These plans, as they are completed, are added to the Emergency Management Plan as appendices so that the final product includes all of the identified hazards being expressly addressed and located in an easily referenced location. Each emergency plan binder distributed will contain a complete set of the Comprehensive Emergency Management Plan including the Emergency Management Plan, the four priority plans (emergency public information, emergency social services, evacuation and telecommunications) and hazard-specific preparedness plans.

DECLARATION OF STATE OF LOCAL EMERGENCY

As an appendix to the Emergency Management Plan, it is wise to prepare a draft Declaration of a State of Local Emergency. If an emergency develops to the point where such will actually be declared, the constraints of the moment would not allow one to produce a carefully worded and all-inclusive declaration. Therefore, it is prudent to prepare a draft declaration where either the blanks can simply be filled in or, if one needs to be customized to the situation, the appropriate wording and format can be copied from the draft. This will aid in avoiding problems of hastily prepared declarations which may not be legally complete or correct since this declaration is being made to take on extraordinary powers for which the local government may be closely scrutinized, and held accountable for, once the emergency has passed.

EVACUATION ORDER AND NOTICE OF EVACUATION ORDER

The same reasoning for having a draft Declaration of a State of Local Emergency applies to having a draft Evacuation Order and draft Notice of Evacuation Order as separate appendices. Time constraints and the pressure of the moment may not allow proper time or clarity of thought to produce the mandatory evacuation order and its required notice. Again, these documents must be beyond reproach as the local government may be held accountable for a range of potential legal actions resulting from the forced removal of residents from their homes.

MUTUAL AID AGREEMENTS

Mutual aid agreements are agreements for support negotiated between two, usually neighboring, jurisdictions. Typically these involve fire departments but can be negotiated for any resources the two parties feel are of value, since most mutual aid agreements are reciprocal. This may include emergency supplies, alternate Emergency Operations Center locations, emergency social services volunteers, etc. A great deal of time and effort is expended on negotiating mutual aid agreements, so they should be kept in a location where they can both be referenced and made known to users of the Emergency Management Plan. As an appendix to the Plan, they are then kept with the other components of the overall Comprehensive Emergency Management Plan and, in keeping with the annual review of these other components, are then available for some form of systematic review or renegotiation to ensure their continued relevance and effectiveness.

COMMUNITY RESOURCE INVENTORY

The final appendix should be a community resource inventory. While each sub-plan has its list of resources relevant to the purpose and nature of that plan, a larger more comprehensive resource list should be kept. The complexity of this list will be determined by the size of the community. Smaller communities stand a chance of possibly developing an inventory that includes most things available, such as heavy equipment, generators, buses, etc., whereas such a comprehensive job may very well be impossible in a larger community.

Nonetheless, the principle is to note in an appendix the item, its contact person, its location and what would be required to transport it. This list can include anything the Emergency Program Coordinator or members of the Emergency Program Planning Committee feel would be necessary to include. Such an inventory is a dynamic list and requires updating on some systematic basis. While it is a great deal of work to compile and keep current, it could very well prove to be one of the most valuable resources during a time of emergency.

Emergency Management Plan Checklist

	Table of Contents
	Distribution List
	Mayor's Endorsement
	Authority
	Scope
	Authorization
	Line of Succession
	Activation
	Role of the Emergency Operations Center
	Hazard Analysis
	Public Information
	Annual Review
	Emergency Operations Center
	Purpose
	Location
	Staffing
	Prolonged Operations
	Equipment
	Liability Issues
	State of Local Emergency
	Declaration of State of Local Emergency
	Powers of Council during a State of Local
Emergency	
	Cancellation of a State of Local Emergency
	Appendices
	Responsibilities During and After an Emergency
	Emergency Telephone Call Out List
	Emergency Public Information Plan
	Emergency Social Services Plan
	Evacuation Plan
	Emergency Telecommunications Plan
	Hazard-Specific Preparedness Plans
	Declaration of State of Local Emergency
	Evacuation Order
	Notice of Evacuation Order
	Mutual Aid Agreement(s)
	Community Resource Inventory

EMERGENCY PUBLIC INFORMATION PLAN

The Emergency Public Information Plan details the local government's concept for conveying relevant information about an actual or anticipated emergency to its residents in a timely fashion. This plan should be a tool ready to be put into use on a moment's notice when the Emergency Operations Center deems it to be necessary. Usually any extraordinary situation, especially when the Emergency Operations

Center is deployed, will necessitate the passing along of information to the public and, therefore, the use of this Plan.

The Emergency Public Information Plan is structured much like the Emergency Management Plan and is done so largely for the consistency of format. It does not contain the great detail of the Emergency Management Plan in areas such as legal authority and the establishment of the Emergency Program Planning Committee, but immediately gets to the point under general headings such as purpose, scope, *Concept of Operations*, objectives, and activation. Beyond this are specifics of this particular plan such as establishing the role of the Public Information Officer, the call out procedure for those involved with this plan, duties and immediate action checklists for those involved, the establishment of an Emergency Public Information Center and the equipment necessary to operate that function.

The actual contents of each Emergency Public Information Plan will vary among local governments as a function of the way they wish to handle media releases, the existing public relations structure of the organization, and how the media will be involved with reporting on the emergency.

The purpose of such a plan is clearly to keep residents of the jurisdiction apprised of the extent of an emergency and any special precautions they need to take by providing relevant and timely information. The scope of the plan refers to types of emergencies to which the plan applies. Most simply, the plan could be called upon for any type or size of emergency when the public information component is called for. Alternatively, the plan could involve certain actions which may only be justified in larger-scale emergencies such as large call centers. The *Concept of Operation* is a concise paragraph which states the vision of how the plan will fulfil its purpose. In the case of emergency public information, it could generally be stated that the release of information and the focal point for questions would be the Emergency Public Information Center under the control of the Public Information Officer.

The objectives of the plan reflect the priorities of the local government in this area and should be simple, achievable and measurable. Objectives could include the timely deployment of the Emergency Public Information Center, prompt proactive liaison with the media outlets, a timeframe for the scheduled release of media releases, to attempt to anticipate the needs of both residents and the media by providing fact sheets, backgrounders, "how to" guides, etc. Activation needs to be addressed so when it is determined the Emergency Public Information Plan needs to be used, the contact person is notified and the rapid deployment of the plan occurs promptly thereafter. It should state who is authorized to activate the plan, a short checklist of whom else then to contact and actions to be taken for the set up of the Emergency Public Information Center.

A brief section on who needs to be called out should be included. This will vary with the size of the local government but will indicate such persons as those employed in the Emergency Public Information Center, volunteers for a call center if needed, and the Mayor and Chief Administrative Officer. The Mayor and Chief Administrative Officer should be responsible for making the actual statements to the media as residents lend greater credibility to information in time of strife when it comes from the top. Detail on the location, set up and organization of the Emergency Public Information Center should also be included. This will detail how the media will be handled, what information will be released, on whose authority that will take place and how it will occur. Alternate locations for the Emergency Public Information Center, staffing for prolonged operations, and accreditation and identification of members of the media are other issues to be addressed.

Appendices to this plan should include a list of the relevant media outlets and a twenty-four hour emergency contact number for the respective news directors, a telephone contact list for those involved with either the operation of the Emergency Public Information Center or in making "on camera" appearances, a ready-made news release which can be photocopied and have an appropriate message written or typed in, and a tip sheet of dos and don'ts when dealing with the media. The latter may be particularly beneficial for those in alternate positions not possessing any media relations training.

This plan should be concise and all-inclusive. For those responsible for emergency public information, they will need to know the basic structure and parameters of how information will be released in order to effectively do their jobs, and not detail on emergency procedures outside of their realm as expert in information dissemination.

Emergency Public Information Plan Outline

Purpose
Annual Review
Scope
Concept of Operation
Objectives
Activation
Callout Procedure
Public Information Officer
    Duties
    Immediate Action Checklist
Emergency Public Information Center
    Public Information Clerk
    Location and Alternate
    Equipment
    Layout
    Prolonged Operations
    Media Accreditation
Call Center
    Location
    Volunteers
    Technical Issues
Appendices
    Media Outlets and Contacts
    EPIC Staff Contact Numbers
    News Release Template

EMERGENCY SOCIAL SERVICES PLAN

The Emergency Social Services Plan is one of the most important aspects of an Emergency Management Plan and the Comprehensive Emergency Management Plan. It is also one of the most complex and all-inclusive sub-plans and is the one which will probably have the greatest impact on individuals during an emergency.

There are basically four spheres of responsibility to be addressed in the Emergency Social Services Plan:

- the care of displaced persons at reception centers;

- the provision of registration and inquiry services for tracking those displaced persons;
- providing food in support of on-scene responders and the Emergency Operations Center and Emergency Public Information Center staffs during prolonged operations; and,
- assisting in the provision of critical incident stress debriefings.

Critical to achieving success in these areas is a good Emergency Social Services Director. Attributes which constitute a good Director are of course subjective, however, the individual must be highly motivated, resourceful and well trained. The emergency social services function cannot be done by one person, but, in fact, requires a large team of volunteers of which the Director acts as the quarterback. Having the right person in the job will make a noticeable difference to the smoothness and effectiveness of this function. Training is an important issue which the local government must be prepared to support, not only for the Director, but also for other volunteers. Many Provincial, State and Federal emergency management agencies offer such training in addition to emergency social services associations and the Red Cross. Available training generally ranges from general management for the Director to task-specific management, such as managing reception centers, to the necessary skills to ensure smooth functioning, such as registration and inquiry training and basic counselling.

The plan the Director is responsible for assembling must be flexible to accommodate a variation in the scale of emergencies and the subsequent level of deployment required, as well as being aware of the regional scale which may see displaced persons sent out of the community or sent in from other jurisdictions.

Three elements are necessary to ensure success in achieving this flexibility and should be considered in developing the Emergency Social Services Plan. These are:
- adequate facilities in appropriate locations around the community;
- the ability to acquire sufficient quantity and quality of the necessary supplies such as food, bedding, clothing, etc.; and,
- reliable and efficient communications.

Facilities should be strategically located around the community to minimize travel time of evacuees, and to make it convenient for evacuees to register even if they will not be making use of the reception center. The facilities should be spread out sufficiently to avoid a disproportionate impact on reception centers by a particular emergency, as might happen if reception centers were concentrated.

The ability to acquire sufficient supplies to support the operation of reception centers is obviously critical to their success and can provide the limiting constraint where not available. One option is stockpiling of emergency supplies.

Finally, communications is important to effective coordination. Amateur Radio volunteers should be coordinated, in conjunction with the Emergency

Telecommunications Plan, to be stationed at all reception centers, the Emergency Operations Center and any other transportation or supply marshalling point which figures prominently in the plan. This will greatly assist in the placing of orders for resources and tracking dispatches. Packet Radio, digital communications allowing computer to computer data transfer, is an excellent means of communicating names and lists, and readily suits the needs of most emergency social services plans.

Given a responsive Emergency Social Service Plan and implementation as outlined, this will assist in accommodating a number of scenarios, specifically evacuating one part of the community to another, evacuating large sections of the population to points outside the community, and accommodating evacuees from other communities affected by an emergency. This will provide the flexibility necessary to adapt to a number of scenarios. A more thorough estimate of the likelihood of such eventualities can be fostered by having the Director involved in the community risk assessment which will provide important background for the strategic location of reception centers and emergency stockpiles in order to facilitate a system of fallback positions if more vulnerable sites are in fact affected by an emergency.

The Emergency Social Services Plan, therefore, should have a focus on facilities as its core. These should be "neighborhood" facilities which are readily identifiable to local residents as an obvious place to congregate. Several considerations should be taken into account such as the size of the facility compared to the population of the designated neighbourhood, the vulnerability of the particular structure *vis a vis* potential hazards, and the nature of the emergencies which may occur in that neighborhood. For example, it may be a centrally located facility that would remain safe from, and appropriate in the case of, emergencies such as flooding or wildfires which may occur in more isolated "fingers" of the neighborhood, or in the case of a "one-time," non-residual emergency such as an earthquake. However, if it is vulnerable to area-wide emergencies such as extreme weather, explosion or hazardous materials, provision must be made for congregating out of the neighborhood in an unaffected, safe area.

Thus, the plan requires the placement of facilities around the community to provide this "layered defense." Facilities, once located, should be able to provide for the sleeping, washing and basic recreation of a large number of potential users. Community halls and recreation facilities are appropriate choices while the use of schools should be carefully and critically reviewed as reception centers may continue to house people for prolonged periods and would hinder the "return to normal" and the resumption of regular classes.

Sufficient and properly trained volunteers should be the second focus of the plan. A well-coordinated staff is the backbone to achieving the goals of the plan. Volunteers will open the facilities, conduct the registration and inquiry for evacuees and will prepare and distribute the support services, such as food, bedding, health services and counselling. Coordination of volunteers is a responsibility of the Director's team of facility and support managers. Everyone should have an assigned task and location to ensure maximum efficiency.

Resources will be the third focus of the plan. Based on an assessment of the potential number of evacuees to be housed, food, bedding and clothing sources must be identified in sufficient quantities. This may entail an appendix to this plan listing the various suppliers of each and telephone information for after-hours contact.

Finally, as with each of the other plans, the activation of this plan should be addressed. This will deal with who has the authority to activate the plan and who will determine what scale this activation will be at. Part of this will also include an appendix listing contact information for the volunteers.

While this provides an overview of the Emergency Social Services Plan, the Emergency Program Coordinator should not lose sight of either the importance or complexity of this plan and the need for an appropriately trained individual to coordinate this effort if it is to be truly successful. The development of the Emergency Social Services Plan should run concurrently with the development of the Emergency Management Plan so that it is available for use once the main issues of general emergency response coordination are in place.

Emergency Social Services Plan Outline

Purpose
Annual Review
Scope
Concept of Operation
Objectives
Activation
Callout Procedure
Emergency Lodging
Emergency Feeding
Emergency Clothing
Registration and Inquiry
Individual and Family Services
    Support Agencies and Personnel
Reception Center Administration
Communications
Additional Supplies
Facilities
    Primary
    Secondary
Supplies
Extended Operations
Closing Down

EVACUATION PLAN

Like the other plans, the Evacuation Plan starts off with a S*statement of Purpose* (i.e., to remove residents from harm's way), *Scope* (geared towards general applicability in any scale of emergency) and the *Concept of Operation* (the vision of how this plan will be employed, e.g. likely sources of emergency necessitating evacuation). Beyond this, the plan varies in its content to meet local requirements.

Two types of evacuation should be considered: *immediate* evacuation in the event of rapidly developing emergencies, and *anticipatory* evacuation in the event of slowly progressing emergencies. Given these two generalized types of evacuations, the plan should address how each type of evacuation is ordered.

In **immediate evacuations** common sense on the part of residents may save lives in the minutes following an emergency. An apparent safety radius will establish itself even by the time first responders arrive. The plan must formalize among the response agencies how a proper and effective safety radius will be established. Given the hazardous materials training of most fire departments, this is probably the best-trained body to decide this in consultation with various reference sources. Other first responders must be made aware of the potential for collateral effects of the initial emergency such as pooling, down-wind effects, explosion potential of liquid and gas leaks, and BLEVEs (boiling liquid evaporating vapor explosion), for example.

The plan should recognize and support the formal power of both police and fire to order immediate evacuations for safety reasons, as well as providing support to those such field officers, in whose best judgement, certain actions are necessary for public safety even if it assumes some risk (albeit a calculated and good risk). If an emergency evolves beyond the scope of the actions taken to this point, the on-scene commander must consult with the Emergency Operations Center (assumed to be set up as soon as possible after the emergency to attend to the evacuation and site support) to consider the use of a State of Local Emergency to use those extraordinary powers to expand the area of mandatory evacuation.

The other type of evacuation is the **anticipatory evacuation** where a slowly progressing phenomenon will make an emergency imminent within the jurisdiction of the local government. Such an evacuation usually has two stages: initially a voluntary evacuation warning for those wishing to evacuate early, and a mandatory evacuation (in British Columbia issued under a State of Local Emergency) once the emergency is critically imminent.

Given the two scenarios, the expansion of an immediate evacuation area or the issuance of a mandatory evacuation order in an anticipatory evacuation, all of which should be addressed in an early part of the plan discussing these two options, the remaining steps are common to both. Notification must be given to residents. Options include use of the Emergency Public Information Plan to get word to local media outlets, police/fire/public works mobile public address systems, or door-to-door volunteers. The most successful way to do this which ensures little gets overlooked is to go door-to-door and mark each house as having been notified, e.g. bright flagging tape on the door or mailbox. Technology has provided local governments with another notification option through the use of an automatic telephone call-out system. The telephone numbers in a certain area can be determined which are then dialled automatically and a recorded message conveyed to the recipient.

Evacuation routes require some forethought, and maps of such should form an appendix to the Plan. The major transportation routes through and around the jurisdiction should be identified to direct any movement efficiently to a safe area. Depending on the topography and other development constraints such as rail lines and bodies of water, it is probably wise to identify logical sub-areas of the jurisdiction which lend themselves to an appropriate scale where evacuation routes out of that area can be identified and analyzed for sufficiency of numbers, capacity and any possible limitations or constraints. Also, anticipation must be given to the time of year an evacuation may occur and appropriate resources made available, e.g. snow removal.

Having identified these routes, the police and public works can develop additional aspects of the Evacuation Plan covering marking and clearing the routes, and traffic control. In this analysis exercise, bottlenecks and other problems areas such as low-lying underpasses subject to flooding can be identified.

Having evacuated residents in immediate danger, the next task for the plan to anticipate is security of the area. This will involve police patrols to prevent people from entering into and roaming around the evacuation area. This particular role has two aspects which involve the nature of the evacuation: police may not, in fact, be able to patrol the area if the evacuation is due to down-wind effects of a leak, or may be able to patrol an area if special equipment is made available to overcome the nature of the emergency, e.g. boats or snowmobiles. Obviously, security of the evacuated area can only be provided where it is safe to do so.

Evacuation Plan Outline

Purpose
Annual Review
Scope
Concept of Operation
Objectives
Activation
Initial Response
Notification
Security
Evacuation Routes
Immediate Evacuation
Anticipatory Evacuation
    Voluntary
    Mandatory
Immobile Persons
Appendices
    Route Clearing Heavy Equipment
    Mass Transportation Resources
    Maps
        Major Transportation Routes
        Designated Evacuation Routes

The Evacuation Plan should anticipate disabled and immobile persons. Keeping an accurate and up-to-date list could be a difficult undertaking, so the ability of the Plan to deal with them as they are discovered should be the objective. In notifying residents through going door-to-door and a disabled or immobile person is identified, that person's evacuation should be facilitated with the cooperation of neighbors, where practical. Where special handling or specialized medical attention is required, an ambulance service will need to be involved.

Finally mass transportation should be a contingency within the Evacuation Plan. Possible scenarios include one where personal vehicles cannot be used, a large institution must be evacuated, a heavily urbanized area where car ownership may be low, or minimizing congestion is necessary because of constraints on some evacuation routes. The plan should have emergency contact capabilities with the transit system, school district transportation staff, and private operators. Appendices to the Plan should include a list of resources possibly required, such as snow clearing equipment and buses, and the contact information for that operator, and maps of the major transportation routes and sub-area evacuation routes.

The final destination of any evacuees, their registration, care, feeding and longer-term needs, are then provided for in the Emergency Social Services Plan.

EMERGENCY TELECOMMUNICATIONS PLAN

The ability to communicate during an emergency is the single most important factor in determining the overall success or failure of response operations. To ensure communications are reliable and open at all times to key locations in the response phase, a comprehensive **Emergency Telecommunications Plan** must be in place to address modes of communications, their capacity and their vulnerabilities.

The "front end" of most emergency plans should contain standard introductory and performance criteria, such as Purpose, Scope, *Concept of Operation* and Objectives.

The *Purpose* of an Emergency Telecommunications Plan is to provide an uninterrupted means of communications between all critical sites during all phases of preparing for, responding to, and recovering from, an emergency. The *Scope* of the plan should be such that it is applicable to any scale of emergency where communications could be compromised and alternate means necessary. The *Concept of Operation* would see this plan providing for: effective and efficient communications to facilitate the response; telecommunications established and maintained to the provincial/state emergency program; and, establish a resource list of supporting supplies. *Objectives* would contain any measurements chosen to be employed in assessing the success of the plan (e.g. deployment times, rapid establishment of all systems, annual exercises, etc.)

Beyond this, the Emergency Telecommunications Plan is customized to each local jurisdiction but should cover some basic common elements.

The role of the Telecommunications Officer should be clarified in an early part of the Plan. However, depending upon the message-handling model selected (to be discussed shortly) the job of the Telecommunications Officer may vary. Ultimately, the Telecommunications Officer is responsible for developing a thorough and workable Emergency Telecommunications Plan. Generally, however, the Telecommunications Officer has two roles, divided between preparedness and response.

In the preparedness phase, the Telecommunications Officer is responsible, under the direction of the Emergency Program Coordinator, for conducting an inventory and assessment of the jurisdiction's existing telecommunications systems, for planning upgrading, compatibility and expanded capacity, and coordinating a common frequency for field use by any, and potentially all, responding agencies. In the response role, the Telecommunications Officer is responsible for communications into, and out of, the Emergency Operations Center, the establishment of communications, and the supply of a trained communicator at locations selected under the Emergency Social Services Plan, e.g. reception centers.

The Telecommunications Officer answers to the Emergency Program Coordinator and responds to, or anticipates, requests for supplementary or alternative telecommunications systems. Further, the Telecommunications Officer is responsible for supervising the communications room. The Telecommunications Officer supports the service radio operators (location to be determined under "message coordination") and directly supervises all Amateur Radio operators. The hallmarks of a good Telecommunications Officer are thorough liaison and planning, developing a cadre of trained and eager Amateur Radio operators, appropriate anticipation of Emergency Operations Center needs, and a smoothly operating communications room. All of these should translate into a workable Emergency Telecommunication Plan.

A summary of the telecommunications systems in the jurisdiction should be articulated noting which agencies have what capabilities, and the degree of interconnectedness and frequency sharing. The general hierarchy of use is telephone, commercial VHF and Amateur Radio. Some electronic mail and instant messaging use in larger and well equipped local governments is being used ahead of telephones. This summary should note the electronic messaging capability and compatibility of each agency or service, the number of telephone, facsimile and data lines servicing each key location (in particular the Emergency Operations Center) and its capacity for expansion; whether or not that agency or service has VHF radio capability, the number of frequencies available, the radio license call sign, whether a repeater is used , the number of base, mobile and portable radios, and the approximate coverage area of each; and, finally, an assessment of the local Amateur Radio capability and the number of trained volunteers.

Message coordination should be addressed and the system to be used must be clearly articulated. Here, the Emergency Program Coordinator, in consultation with the Chief Administrative Officer, must decide what approach to message handling they wish to take. One model would see each Emergency Operations Center participant with either a computer, telephone and radio, or all, at their position in the Emergency Operations Center, perhaps with the assistance of a communicator, controlling their own communications and responsible for maintaining a telecommunications log. This model would see the Amateur Radio back-up capability in a separate communications room.

Conversely, all communication may go through a communication room via numbered message pads to the particular service-specific communicator with the back up Amateur Radio capability all in that same communications room. The former model is preferred as it allows for a freer flow of communications. The potential problem points are enforcing the use of a service telecommunications log and breaking decision-makers away from their service's action for conferences (although this is made easier with the use of a communicator for each service present in the Emergency Operations Center). When the choice of models is made, it should be stated clearly for Emergency Operations Center members to plan towards.

Operational protocol should also be outlined. It is unrealistic, and perhaps unwise, to expect a service dispatch operation to operate any differently in an extreme emergency rather than a "routine" emergency. These emergency service dispatch centers are already designed to operate efficiently under emergency conditions. Given this, the officials from these services present in the Emergency Operations Center will most likely communicate with their respective dispatch center by the most reliable and readily available means, namely the telephone.

Emergency Telecommunications Plan Outline

Purpose
Annual Review
Scope
Concept of Operation
Objectives
Activation
Callout Procedure
Telecommunications Officer
    Duties
    Immediate Action Checklist
Communications Room
    Set-up
    Equipment
    Message Handling Model
    Logs
    Volunteers
    Hierarchy of Use
    Service Protocol
Staffing Remote Locations
Prolonged Operations
Appendices
    Network Diagram
    Frequencies
    Volunteer Contact Information

Usually, in the event of failure or congestion with the telephone system, service radios already in use with that service's field units would be relied upon to pass information between that service representative in the Emergency Operations Center and the respective dispatch office. For each message in or out of the Emergency Operations Center by each service, an entry is required in the service telecommunications log. This not only serves as a reminder to the particular service representative, but also as a historic record of the emergency and as a legal document for possible subsequent litigation. The Amateur Radio operators provide this radio service to those services which may not have a radio system, but usually provide this between the Emergency Operations Center to its reception centers when the telephone system fails or to remote pickets such as dyke patrol or at dam sites.

Towards the end of the plan, mention should be made of the need for annual review, for telecommunications training and the need for a schedule of telecommunication exercises.

Finally, as appendices to this plan, contact numbers and call signs for the Amateur Radio operators and any other volunteers or staff required to fill roles in the Plan should be kept up to date as well as a list of telephone numbers to key offices, buildings, and dispatch centers for reference in setting up and testing communication links, and a network diagram which shows the land/fax/data lines, the frequencies in use and any interconnectedness which (desirably) may exist.

HAZARD-SPECIFIC PREPAREDNESS PLANS

Hazard-Specific Preparedness Plans are the bulk of the overall Comprehensive Emergency Management Plan. After the core Emergency Management Plan and the four generally applicable "priority" plans, the hazard-specific preparedness plans provide the details on responding to a specific type of emergency. Such a plan should exist for each hazard identified in the risk assessment portion of the mitigation phase. Identifying a particular hazard is done for a very obvious reason: unless risk management techniques can address the hazard to the point of it no longer being a threat, a plan should be written to address the specifics of response should that emergency occur.

Given the array of hazards faced by communities, it is difficult to identify one response model to fit all instances. There are, however, a number of points which can be generalized about each plan. Each plan must take into consideration the command and control provisions of the Emergency Management Plan and conform to this vision. Beyond this it is a standalone plan, meaning that it contains all necessary information to respond to that particular type of emergency. The Emergency Program Coordinator may want to keep in mind it is the Emergency Management Plan which gets the decision-makers to the Emergency Operations Center, and the four priority plans may be called on if and when needed, but it is the individual, hazard-specific, preparedness plan that commands the long term attention of the decision-makers. Given this mental guide, the all-inclusive, or stand alone, nature of each hazard-specific preparedness plan can be appreciated.

Each such plan needs to state a purpose and set objectives for what it is attempting to achieve. Objectives are important, for without these there is no measurement instrument with which to assess relative success. Explicit objectives also set out clearly to the decision-makers in the Emergency Operations Center what is intended to be accomplished. A brief section of background information may also be included which will outline the threat assessment and any mitigation efforts. This will provide the Emergency Operations Center with a brief understanding of the threat at hand and what has been done to minimize its impact. This information is valuable to the

Emergency Operations Center and should be reasonably accurate as each plan is reviewed annually for changes.

In keeping with the paradigm being conveyed in this book, the *Scope of Applicability* should also be presented. The philosophy consistently conveyed throughout this work has been the more regularly these plans are relied on for "routine" emergencies, (i.e. those slightly beyond regular occurrences which require an added degree of coordination or extra resources), the greater will be the familiarity with the plan as will be the efficacy of the plan, so that when a major emergency occurs, the plan is simply increased in scale and scope. Hence, scope should address the expandability or modular nature of the plan, meaning it can be used in anything from small emergencies requiring just a bit of extraordinary support to major emergencies where the Incident Command System will see additional resources, or modules, added on to the response effort allowing it to grow to the necessary scale.

The *Concept of Operation* takes the idea of a flexible scale of applicability to practical terms. In a few paragraphs, this is where a response is visualized. It anticipates a regular response by resources of the jurisdiction and the possible inclusion of any additional agencies, such as industrial response bodies where required. It then briefly outlines who else gets involved as the scope of the emergency increases to include mutual aid support, regional, provincial/state and possibly federal assistance.

The next section, *Initial Response*, should put details to the outline identified under *Concept of Operation*. The importance of this section is to cover the initial on-scene assessment by the appropriate agency and may address the potential arrival of other emergency response agencies before the one appropriately trained to make such assessments, e.g., police first to arrive at a hazardous materials spill. Generally, the best approach is to provide immediate action checklists for both responders and Emergency Operations Center members. This will ensure that the necessary basic information is collected and passed back to the Emergency Operations Center in the early stages of an emergency when people may still be trying to come to terms with the situation.

On-scene command must also be addressed so that this is rapidly sorted out. This will state to the Emergency Operations Center who they need to talk to for command and control issues while clarifying at the scene who is to take charge. Part of this topic should also address multiple-agency integration. This will outline how the multiple agencies native to the jurisdiction will work together under a unified command but will also address Incident Command System issues of expansion if an emergency justifies extensive outside support.

Further, the plan should address prolonged operations. It will have to accommodate the changeover of command personnel and the subsequent briefing necessary to accomplish this, in addition to rotating line workers. Such provisions may be quite complicated when they exceed the ability of the normal shift system to accommodate this. At that point mutual aid or staffing assistance from senior levels of government may be required.

Reporting requirements and other situation reports should be stipulated to provide the Emergency Operations Center with regular updates. Other routine management aspects should be provided for, such as the designation of a resource marshalling point, hot zones and rest areas.

Additional resources, generally of a miscellaneous nature, should be identified in an appendix to the plan. Depending on the subject of the plan, additional, larger, unique or bulk equipment/ resources should be identified with complete and accurate contact information.

Finally, a section should be given over to demobilization and "wind-down." A particular site is not simply abandoned after an initial response; Operations are scaled back and equipment released to a point where a site is deemed safe, the problem rectified or a hazard removed. Careful thought should be given to how this occurs right down to the point where the last person departs the site. Issues to be addressed include allowing residents/workers back into the area, patrols or follow-up inspections and a legacy of possible contaminated or uninhabitable areas requiring security patrols or to be cordoned off.

The hazard-specific preparedness plan is an excellent opportunity to brainstorm the response to a particular emergency in full anticipation of its occurrence. A small committee may be formed comprising experts on the topic so that every facet of such a response at different scales can be thought through. Anticipated problems or equipment/resource shortfalls can be addressed well in advance of the emergency and without the pressure of an actual response occurring simultaneously. This then becomes the guide, or script, which will be used by both the Emergency Operations Center and the response agencies to lead them through such an emergency. Ensuring both parties are thinking in the same manner greatly increases the efficiency and effectiveness of emergency response.

Hazard-Specific Preparedness Plans Outline

Purpose
Annual Review
Scope
Concept of Operation
    Objectives
Activation
Threat Assessment
Mitigation Efforts
    Initial Response
Initial Action Checklist
Multiple Agency Integration
Prolonged Operations
    Security
Demobilization
Appendices
    Additional Resources
    Contact Information (including Alternates)

MUTUAL AID AGREEMENTS

Mutual aid agreements serve two purposes: they are a means to provide supplementary resources when those of the local jurisdiction are already committed to the task or the scale of an emergency overwhelms the limited local resources; and, they are a means of securing access to speciality equipment which a neighboring, perhaps larger, jurisdiction may possess.

Such an agreement is negotiated between two or more local governments and specifies the terms and conditions under which such sharing of resources will occur. It is a legal document and is officially sealed by each participant since liability and indemnity responsibilities may be transferred between parties.

Standard mutual aid agreements usually exist between neighboring jurisdiction for the traditional primary response agencies: police, fire and ambulance. As the name implies, these mutual aid agreements are usually reciprocal so parties entering into such agreements must be willing, and able, to support the other party or parties when called upon.

These documents are an important aspect of a local government's emergency planning and will influence its ability to respond to large-scale emergencies. As such, they need to be kept accessible and relevant. Copies of mutual aid agreements should reside both collectively in an appendix to the Emergency Management Plan. Those tied to specific types of emergencies, such as sandbags and pumps for flooding or volunteers for emergency social services tasks, should also be appended to that particular hazard-specific preparedness plan.

These agreements should be kept current with changing conditions, terms and circumstances through an annual review with all parties involved in the agreement. This ensures that they will continue to serve their original purpose to those parties involved.

Mutual aid agreements can serve a valuable and useful role in emergency preparedness and response if they are based upon a realistic assessment of the potential scale of an emergency and the likely availability of the resources called upon. These constraints are typically local, and attempting to negotiate acceptable terms and conditions will determine whether a truly beneficial mutual aid agreement can be created.

COMMUNITY RESOURCE INVENTORY

A community resource inventory is an inventory of those items in the community that could be called upon if and when needed in the preparation for, response to, or recovery from, an emergency. A list of potentially required items accumulated over time may prove to be invaluable to the Emergency Operations Center in addressing an emergency.

Such a listing of resources could prove to be confusing and misleading if not properly organized. A master list should be kept and categorized, such as heavy equipment, service clubs, generators, pumps, buses, etc. This master list should be an appendix to the Emergency Management Plan, while selected portions of this list which may be called upon in particular hazard-specific preparedness plans should be listed as an appendix to those plans.

A community resource inventory is a large and difficult undertaking and is one which inevitably will not be totally accurate. Such a listing cannot be amassed in a short period of time, rather, it evolves and grows over time as resources come and go from the community and are brought to the attention of the Emergency Program Coordinator. However, as with most other aspects of emergency planning, an annual review of this inventory involving telephoning the designated contact person for each item or resource will verify the accuracy of the information and the reliability of securing that resource when needed.

For the purpose of this inventory, the resource should be noted along with the contact person and their telephone number. An alternate contact person should also be noted. The Emergency Program Coordinator must accept this list as being dynamic, that individual listings may come and go throughout the year between annual reviews, and that such a listing will require ongoing updating as intelligence comes to the Coordinator's attention.

Given the difficulty of creating and maintaining such an inventory, its compilation during non-emergency times and the breadth of items included may prove to be an invaluable resource to the Emergency Operations Center when challenged to mount a quick and effective response. The sole purpose of the community resource inventory is to provide access to a wide range of miscellaneous items which may prove valuable given the unpredictable nature of both large and small emergencies. Some needs may be predictable, such as those associated with emergency social services, while others may require significant volumes, e.g. sand and sandbags, and still others may be used in rare circumstances. Nonetheless, the community resource inventory should be designed to satisfy all of these needs.

PERSONAL AND FAMILY PREPAREDNESS AND SAFETY

Personal and family preparedness and safety is a critical element to the successful preparation for, response to, and recovery from, an emergency which most organizations overlook. Local government staff, especially those who occupy critical emergency management roles, cannot constructively contribute to response and recovery operations if their mind is constantly focused upon their own families' safety and well being.

It is in the best interest of every local government to stress that staff adequately prepare their families and homes for a major emergency. Proper personal and family preparedness planning will make it easier for staff to confirm the post-emergency status of their families. Once this is done, staff is free to focus on their emergency response role without being preoccupied with personal concerns.

The American Red Cross and the U.S. Federal Emergency Management Agency have produced an excellent brochure on family emergency preparedness. This brochure has been condensed into the following useful checklist.

Personal and Family Emergency Checklist

Ask the following questions at your local government office:

What hazards threaten the jurisdiction?

How should one prepare for each eventuality?

How would one be warned of such an occurrence?

What are the community evacuation routes?

Is there special assistance for the elderly, disable or immobile persons?

Also investigate:

emergency plans and escape routes at your place of employment

emergency plans at your children's school and facilities where they may attend programs

Create a Family Emergency Plan:

Meet with household members to discuss the dangers of fire, severe weather, earthquakes and other emergencies. Explain how to react to each.

Find the safe spots in your home for each type of emergency.

Discuss what to do about power outages and personal injuries.

Draw a floor plan of your home and mark two escape routes from each room.

Show family members how to shut off the water, gas and electricity at main switches if necessary.

Post emergency telephone numbers near telephones.

Teach children how and when to call 911 or police, fire and ambulance where 911 is not available.

Instruct family members to turn on the radio for emergency information.

Pick one out of the region and one local friend or relative for family members to call if separated during an emergency.

Ensure your children know the out of region contact's telephone number.

Pick two emergency meeting places:

1. A place near your home in case of fire.
2. A place outside your neighbourhood in case you cannot return home after an emergency.

Take a basic first aid and CPR course.

Keep family records in a water and fire-proof container.

Emergency Supplies Kit

a supply of water (one gallon per person per day). Store water in sealed, unbreakable containers. Identify the storage date and replace every six months

a supply of non-perishable packaged or canned food and a non-electric can opener

a change of clothing, rain gear and sturdy shoes

blankets of sleeping bags

a first aid kit and prescription medications

an extra pair of eye glasses

a battery-powered radio, flashlight and plenty of extra batteries

credit cards and cash

an extra set of car keys

a list of family physicians

a list of important family information: the style and serial number of medical devices such as pacemakers

special items for infants, elderly or disabled family members

store these in an easy to carry backpack

Home Hazard Hunt:

repair defective electrical wiring and leaky gas connections

fasten shelves securely and brace overhead light fixtures

place large, heavy objects on lower shelves

hang pictures and mirrors away from beds

strap water heater to wall studs

repair cracks in ceiling or foundation

store pesticides and flammable products away from heat sources

place oily polishing rags or waste in a covered metal can

clean and repair chimneys, flue pipes, vent connectors and gas vents

If You Need to Evacuate:

listen to a battery-powered radio for the location of emergency shelters - follow instructions of local officials

wear protective clothing and sturdy shoes

take your emergency supplies kit

lock your house

use travel routes specified by local officials

If You Have Time:

shut off water, gas and electricity if instructed to do so

let others know when you left and where you are going

make arrangements for pets as animals may not be allowed in public shelters

Prepare an Emergency Car Kit:

battery-powered radio, flashlight and extra batteries

blanket

booster cables

fire extinguisher (5 lb. ABC type)

first aid kit and manual

bottled water and non-perishable high energy foods

map, shovel, flares

tire repair kit and pump

Fire Safety:

plan two escape routes out of each room

practice fire drills at least twice per year

teach family members to stay low to the ground when escaping from a fire

teach family members never to open doors that are hot

install smoke detectors on every level of your home (test monthly and replace batteries annually)

keep a whistle in each bedroom to alert family members in case of fire

check electrical outlets - do not overload outlets

purchase and learn how to use a fire extinguisher (5 lb. ABC type)

have a collapsible latter on each floor of your house

consider installing home sprinklers

* Adapted from the Emergency Preparedness Checklist produced by the American Red Cross and the U.S. Federal Emergency Management Agency

In the event of personal tragedy, alternate staff may be called upon to replace those affected persons so that the emergency management role the persons filled continue to contribute effectively to the response. Local government has an obligation to its residents to provide effective response and recovery operations when an emergency occurs. This cannot be hampered by unfortunate personal circumstances, so proactive measures on the part of the local government to educate their staff in this matter should be undertaken.

EXERCISE OF PLANS

Under the Preparedness Plan, many facets of planning emergency response have come together in formalized plans. Simply documenting the responsibilities, procedures and resources is not sufficient to ensure actual preparedness. The second half of "preparedness" is exercising these plans. A more detailed discussion about the various types of exercises will be undertaken in the last chapter of this book, however, suffice it to say that *a plan is not complete unless it has been tested under controlled circumstances and thoroughly reviewed for errors, omissions, procedures that just don't work, or lack of knowledge on the part of the participants.*

The Emergency Management Plan and its four priority sub-plans should be an exercise priority due to their general applicability to any of the hazard-specific preparedness plans. This ensures that the emergency notification system works, the Emergency Operations Center can be deployed and operates efficiently, evacuation procedures are realistic, sufficient numbers of trained emergency social services volunteers are available, emergency communications function, and information can be readily disseminated to the general public. Hazard-specific preparedness plans should also be exercised in this manner wherever possible although the nature of some of the plans do not easily lend themselves to an exercise without assumptions, scenarios and role playing.

MAINTENANCE AND UPDATE OF PLANS

All emergency plans should be subject to an annual review. Emergency plans contain a great deal of information that is subject to change over the course of a year: organizations are restructured, position titles change, procedures and protocols are revised or changed, equipment is changed as are the skills which go along with its operation, telephone and other contact information changes, and hazards and other conditions within the community change, just to name a few.

It is incumbent on the Emergency Program Coordinator to stay abreast of such changes although this may prove impractical in a large organization without support. Managers in certain key areas of the organization should be aware of what part of their jurisdiction or responsibility is covered under an emergency plan (hopefully they have taken a role in creating that plan and have been involved in exercising that plan). When changes to a part of an organization do occur, those managers should advise the Emergency Program Coordinator so that these changes can be noted for the annual review of that specific plan, or for an interim review and update, if critical. Annual reviews then are coordinated by the Emergency Program Coordinator but should involve a small committee of managers and other key experts from the area covered by the particular plan. The review can either verify that no changes have occurred which affect the plan and it can remain as is, or can note the changes and how the plan needs to be modified to address the change. Once this maintenance is done, the plan should then serve the next year as an effective preparedness plan.

COMPUTER-ASSISTED EMERGENCY MANAGEMENT

Computer hardware and software development has not excluded emergency management from its impact. The evolution of desktop computing power and both custom and "off-the-shelf" software has brought computer-assisted emergency management into the Emergency Operations Center.

Until recently, computer-assisted emergency management has primarily been undertaken by large local governments where powerful servers and custom-designed software have aided in managing large and complex response operations. A variety of software suitable for operating on a single desktop computer or network servers is now available, making this aspect of emergency management well within the resources of most local governments.

In keeping with the pragmatic approach of this book, caution must be exercised in using this type of technology. Where there is a legitimate need for this added resource management tool, some of the potential concerns can be overcome as part of the acquisition and installation process; However, relying on computers and software in times of emergency poses some special considerations, such as ensuring sufficient trained operators are available for all shifts, systems are redundant to avoid the failure of one system or computer, uninterrupted power is available and the system is transportable if an evacuation to an alternate Emergency Operations Center is necessary.

Computer-assisted emergency management can serve a valuable role in emergency planning provided that full and careful thought is put into the weaknesses and vulnerabilities of computers used in adverse circumstances. Many large communities have successfully implemented computer-assisted emergency management systems and will be rewarded when an emergency does occur with fast and efficient resource management. Local governments who fail to fully consider the implications of such a computer-based system will be thrown into disorganization if the system fails during and emergency or worse, the failure of such a system could exacerbate the response effort and possibly cause further damage, injuries or loss of life.

A detailed review of the rapidly evolving market of computer-based emergency management software is not within the scope of this book. Having identified some of the weaknesses of technology-based solutions, individual local governments can assess the market for the proper product for their needs and address the weaknesses during installation.

KEY POINTS

- Preparedness is the opportunity to pre-plan for anticipated emergencies
- Modular approach to compiling the plan allows for iterations of increasing detail
- Preparedness plans exist at all levels of government
- The emergency spectrum ranges from small and routine to the catastrophic
- Construction of the overall Preparedness Plan is broken down into prioritized manageable "sub-plans"
- The Emergency Management Plan is the "hub" of the overall Preparedness Plan and deals with issues of general management common to any emergency response
- The Emergency Management Plan is followed by four priority plans: emergency social services, emergency public information, evacuation and emergency telecommunications
- Subcommittees of the Emergency Program Planning Committee containing specific expertise are struck to develop each of the individual sub-plans
- Emergency public information is critical in order to keep residents informed and aware of the impact and evolving response
- Emergency social services will account for evacuated residents and provide food and shelter as needed
- Evacuation removes residents from harms way either under immediate or anticipatory evacuation
- Communications between the Emergency Operations Center and the site of the emergency, between the Emergency Operations Center and reception centers, and the Emergency Operations Center and the next higher level of authority are necessary prerequisites for a successful response
- Hazard-specific preparedness plans provide specific detail for responding to identified and inevitable hazards
- Mutual aid agreements can provide supplementary or specialized equipment
- Community resource inventory provides a quick- reference list of a range of support items
- Personal and family preparedness is the best "return on investment" by fostering a degree of self-sufficiency
- Troubleshooting of plans/ procedures and instilling retention of their contents are best accomplished through exercises
- Plan maintenance must be an annual event
- A recent proliferation of software packages has fostered computer-assisted emergency management

---

[1] Emergency Program Act, RSBC 1996, Ch. 111.

4

RESPONSE

Response is initiated upon a sudden event or the slow onset of an imminent event. The former is the opportunity for planning, training and exercising to pay off with quick and well-executed immediate actions, while the later allows for time to set up and prepare resources. Nonetheless, certain actions need to occur nearly automatically once an emergency has occurred which are based solely on pre-planning. Major emergencies are not the time to apply ad hoc planning.

MEETING THE IMMEDIATE NEEDS

The response phase of *Comprehensive Emergency Management* is the least controllable and most hectic. It is the phase when all the pre-planning is put to the test, and both the Emergency Program Coordinator and the local government are rewarded as a well-executed plan unfolds nearly automatically – or, are horrified at the gaps overlooked in the planning process.

The execution of most Comprehensive Emergency Management Plans is always a learning opportunity and presents a chance to further refine the plan at the post-emergency review. Bear in mind that no plan is perfect, and improvement is continuual. While learning and improvement are expected, the response phase does not permit time for thorough analysis before *ad hoc* decisions are made. Therefore, fully capitalizing on any opportunity to pre-plan all aspects of the Preparedness Plan is critical. Failing to do so is a severe oversight.

The best-case scenario in the response phase is the deployment of an Emergency Operations Center which is ready with the four priority plans of general applicability (Emergency Social Services, Evacuation, Emergency Telecommunications, Emergency Public Information) to be called upon as necessary, while the response agencies rely upon their hazard-specific preparedness plans for on-scene guidance. Likewise, the Emergency Operations Center follows the execution of a hazard-specific preparedness plan and anticipates the needs of the field units as well as responding promptly to their extraordinary requests. Having these documents in place inspires confidence that most aspects have been addressed and allow for more time to look at extraordinary events as they arise. If not all such plans are in place, an element of disorganization is injected into the Emergency Operations Center and time taken in reacting to such events detracts from other proactive measures a properly prepared Emergency Operations Center should be considering.

THE NATURE OF RESPONSE

Response can be initiated either upon impact, a term used to describe a crash, explosion, fire or a natural event occurrence, or upon an imminent event such as a flood, forest fire, blizzard, tsunami, etc. The latter case allows for the early establishment of the Emergency Operations Center and the readiness of emergency services and other response agencies anticipated to be needed at impact. This warning period allows for what should be a reasonably smooth and coordinated response.

The former, where major emergencies arrive unannounced, do not allow for a smooth deployment of response resources: An incident has occurred and everything a local government can throw at it is needed *now*. Emergency response agencies, traditionally identified as police, fire and ambulance, deal with such response times on a daily basis for small-scale, "routine" emergencies and generally work well together when an emergency is manageable by those initially dispatched. It is when the scale of the emergency is such that multiple units are involved from each service, and coordination within each service is required in addition to inter-service coordination, that confusion is inevitable and a system is required to select an incident commander. This system must be known to all and its principles, and procedures adhered to.

The system which has emerged as the most effective multi-agency coordination model is the Incident Command System. This system, which has emerged from the United States where forest fire fighting has traditionally involved many agencies, espouses a command and management system with common terminology and communication capabilities as fundamental aspects.

In large-scale response scenarios, a senior officer from one of the response agencies will assume command of the site and appoint other senior persons to key roles such as safety, planning and operations officers. The incident commander is responsible for all aspects of combating the emergency *at the site*.

Given that the emergency is of the order that has necessitated the response agencies to go beyond small-scale, "routine" emergency coordination to a larger, more integrated coordination and command body, the local government where the emergency is occurring most likely will have a full or partial deployment of its Emergency Operations Center. The role of the Emergency Operations Center in the response phase is to support the incident commander by coordinating the provision of resources required at the scene and to remove and care for persons ordered evacuated from the immediate area.

Effective response actions must begin to occur immediately after the emergency has occurred. Response agencies are experts in this type of work and meet this expectation in nearly all cases. Generally most emergencies are of the magnitude that there are usually sufficient resources within a particular service or between combined services to deal with most scenarios. In rare circumstances the emergency will overwhelm the combined responding agencies and a call for assistance will be made to the local government. By this time the Emergency Operations Center should be established to receive such a request (the speed with which the Emergency Operations Center is deployed depends upon initial reports from the scene of the extent of the incident) and to secure these additional resources.

Primary response agencies (to which public works should be added), being the professionals in their respective areas, generally have internal plans for dealing with fire, explosion, crowd control, civil unrest and multiple-casualty emergencies. The role of the Emergency Operations Center to support these agencies in large-scale emergencies is to provide resources those agencies are not capable of seeking out or where extraordinary powers are required to control the public or to obtain certain items. In the preparedness phase, lists of resources were identified for this purpose as were mutual aid agreements negotiated to provide extra resources in those rare events which exceed the local capability.

From the Emergency Program Coordinator's perspective, very little can be done in the initial stage of response except ensure those response agencies do have internal plans for limited-scale "routine" emergencies and know who to contact when there is the slightest indication an emergency may escalate dramatically. Proper and thorough planning in the preparedness phase should allow the next steps to occur almost automatically. When one of the persons listed to authorize deployment of the Emergency Operations Center is contacted and the decision is made to fully or partially deploy the Emergency Operations Center, the telephone contact list should allow for all the necessary staff to be quickly contacted and the rapid set-up of the Emergency Operations Center (if not an already dedicated room) once they start to arrive. Following this, depending on the requests, additional equipment can be ordered, evacuations ordered, mutual aid agreements executed and press releases prepared, all of which are provided for in either the Emergency Management Plan or hazard-specific preparedness plan.

Under this typical scenario the situation moves from the unknown to rapid response and assessment, to a request for additional support. Where that support is required, the Emergency Operations Center comes into play and coordinates that support until the emergency is fully addressed.

MUTUAL AID

Mutual aid agreements are negotiated between one or more adjacent emergency response agencies, e.g. between fire departments, police departments or ambulance services/companies, to provide those resources when called upon in extreme cases where all local resources become committed to the emergency. These are negotiated in advance and address such elements as how many units and staff the supplying local government can spare without compromising its own protection or safety, matters of financial compensation and liability coverage, replacement of damaged equipment, response times and notification requirements.

When called upon the supplying local government units may either be involved in actual response or to provide standby for other "routine" emergencies which the host service cannot attend. It is considered advisable to put in place as many mutual aid agreements as possible since those local governments being relied upon for support may also have their own internal needs, finite resources, and may also be affected by the emergency. Multiple mutual aid agreements should ensure that a sufficient degree of support will be available in most circumstances.

Obviously a cost is incurred to the requesting local government when such a request is made. Therefore, such requests must be made by top local government officials. Such powers may be delegated to the head of a response agency, the Fire Chief or Police Chief for example, in those cases where an Emergency Operations Center is not established or, more likely, where urgency is of the essence. Senior local government officials in the Emergency Operations Center must give unquestioning support to the incident commander and not question such requests, rather, to provide this support and to understand and track such expenditures.

SPECIALIZED EQUIPMENT

The emergency necessitating the support of an Emergency Operations Center can be one of many unique emergencies presenting an extraordinary situation. Extraordinary emergencies may require drastic remedies. These may involve highly innovative techniques or "brute force" which is made possible through special equipment. It is the role of the Emergency Operations Center to support the site, and hopefully thorough preparedness by the Emergency Program Planning Committee has provided resource lists covering a wide variety of such equipment. It is impossible to anticipate every scenario and provide a listing of every possible resource which may be requested. Resource lists should be kept for the most commonly needed implements or supplies. In the response phase such requests may include large volumes of sand or fill, firefighting foam, heavy equipment such as excavators and bulldozers, cranes, high-volume pumps, generators, helicopters, etc.

These resources may be critical components in the initial response to an emergency in order to avoid further spread or contamination, or just to provide a proper assessment of the situation. If it is determined to be necessary by the incident commander it should be provided. The Emergency Operations Center and the Emergency Program Coordinator must be prepared for such requests, hopefully having been anticipated in advance with a listing already prepared or by being adept at tracking down such equipment.

EMERGENCY PUBLIC INFORMATION

As indicated under the preparedness phase, emergency public information is a critical aspect of successful emergency management. Simply put, people want to know what has happened and what is being done about it. "Routine" emergencies normally handled within the scope of day-to-day operations of response agencies are expected in everyday life in an urban environment and handled as the various media outlets choose depending on how busy of a news day it has been.

Major emergencies necessitate a proactive approach on the part of the local government who must contact the media outlets, invite them to a briefing location and provide the message that needs to get out to the public. The planning efforts in this regard made by the local government should also happen almost automatically. In general, any emergency necessitating the deployment of the Emergency Operations Center probably involves the scale of emergency that will concern residents. This concern must be addressed by the Emergency Operations Center through regular information bulletins to the media and, increasingly common, via a call center.

Provisions made for contacting the media and for the establishment of a call center should be activated immediately by the Public Information Officer once he/she is notified of the emergency. Other decision-makers within the Emergency Operations Center will be supporting the site in combating the emergency while the Public Information Officer invokes the Emergency Public Information Plan. As noted earlier, this plan encompasses the immediate actions for the Public Information Officer and should contain all the necessary media contact information, templates for news releases, and directions for establishing the call center.

Human psychology tells us that in an emergency, fear and confusion make addressing an emergency and its subsequent recovery extremely difficult. Informed and organized victims seem to be able to tolerate adverse circumstances better and longer when they are aware of what has happened to them, what the scale of the emergency is, how they can address their immediate needs, and how long recovery is anticipated to take. Therefore, it is in the best interest of the local government to meet the challenge of emergency public information head-on and plan for its near automatic deployment in the response phase.

EMERGENCY SOCIAL SERVICES

As with emergency public information, an emergency of the scale that necessitates the deployment of the Emergency Operations Center is bound to have some human elements to it which will need to be addressed. The emergency social services Director will be part of the Emergency Operations Center and will have control over the deployment of the Emergency Social Services Plan once the impact of the emergency has been determined. Only after a thorough appreciation of the situation can it be determined which parts of the Emergency Social Services Plan need to be activated.

The scale of activation may be limited to temporary shelter (one or two days), feeding and clothing for a limited number of people affected by a modest emergency, or may involve the evacuation, registration, sheltering, feeding, clothing and counselling of large numbers of people for perhaps several weeks. This range of possible response scenarios requires the Emergency Social Services Plan to be highly flexible and modular in its ability to expand from a limited scale to a major undertaking. The key to a successful Emergency Social Services Plan is the identification of suitable quantities of the necessary resources, large numbers of trained volunteers, and good communications. All of these figure prominently in the compilation of the Emergency Social Services Plan under the preparedness phase. Resource lists will include a wide variety of support groups and agencies, facilities of different capacities in different locations, volunteers trained in properly caring for displaced persons and the subsequent registration and inquiry tasks, and finally reliable communications between sites, such as Amateur Radio, to ensure that lists of names and requests for further support are accurately and immediately relayed.

RESPONSE SUMMARY

Three aspects of response should stand out clearly: *support the site*, *provide information to the public*, and *tend to the people affected by the emergency*. These aspects are not the end of the emergency, as the lengthy recovery phase is to follow. It is, however, the action that will meet the immediate needs and allow the source of danger to be neutralized quickly and as safely as possible. By far, the lengthiest and most difficult aspect of a major emergency is the recovery phase where the community and local government must now pick up the pieces and carry on.

Key Points

- Avoid *ad hoc* responses
- Use "normal times" to pre-plan for specific hazards
- Response ranges from "routine" types of events to those requiring extensive coordination and support
- Incident Command System is the multi-agency coordination model of choice
- The role of the Emergency Operations Center is to support the incident commander and care for evacuees
- Mutual aid agreements can be negotiated by a variety of agencies
- Resource lists of special equipment can rapidly identify suppliers of unique or bulk resources which may be required
- Major emergencies necessitate a proactive cooperation with media outlets
- Residents affected by an emergency can cope better when informed of the circumstances of the event
- Persons affected or displaced by an emergency may need the benefits of the Emergency Social Services Plan
- Three important aspects: site support, public information and social services

5

RECOVERY

> *There are three fundamental aspects of any organization which require attention in the post-emergency period in order to resume something resembling normal operation: staff, facilities and service (technology and operations). Recovery will be facilitated much more readily and lead to speedier and predictable results if these elements are pre-planned. Staff will need special attention after a major emergency as will local government facilities and the services offered by staff at these locations.*

IS IT POSSIBLE TO RETURN SERVICE, FACILITIES AND PEOPLE TO "NORMAL"?

Recovery is a rather ill defined aspect of *Comprehensive Emergency Management*. As a concept, we know what recovery is, what it involves and when it should occur. However, once the Emergency Program Coordinator starts to contemplate recovery and all it entails, it becomes a more difficult concept to define in clear terms.

Some authorities on emergency management state that recovery starts at impact – the time the emergency actually occurs – while others draw a clear distinction between response and recovery. In the latter conceptualization, recovery is not formally commenced until the response phase is "in-hand" or "under control." Even these terms, in-hand and under control, lack precise definition: is the entire emergency under control or just parts or areas of it, have the flames only been knocked down or is mop-up completed, or has the emergency been contained and the evacuees returned home or do they remain in evacuation centers?

It is a difficult task to resolve these definitional problems with any consistency so it is not worth attempting. In reality, recovery involves a bit of both concepts enumerated by emergency management authorities: some parts of recovery do commence at impact while others must wait until response operations have proceeded to various points. In an attempt to bring at least a little clarity to when recovery operations begin once response activities have the emergency in-hand, it is better to view this transition as a winding down of operations. Therefore, as personnel are released from response duties, facilities are once again accessible (or approachable), equipment released from service, and customers once again expect service, then the various aspects of recovery can be commenced. It is best to visualize this transition in this "winding down" concept as the aforementioned "getting back to normal" elements will occur at different times depending on the scale and scope of the emergency.

SERVICE CONTINUATION PLANNING

Service Continuation Planning is a critical aspect of recovery planning and overall *Comprehensive Emergency Management* at the local level. Where the Emergency Management Plan and the hazard-specific preparedness plans address the actual emergency and its cause, service continuation planning assumes a worst-case scenario emergency *will* occur and addresses maintaining services as close to normal as possible, or restoring services in a timely manner after an emergency. It is an opportunity to make as many decisions as possible in advance of an emergency rather than under the stress of an unfolding emergency when many other things preoccupy the Emergency Program Coordinator.

DEFINITION

Service continuation planning, as it applies to local government's ability to continue to provide services throughout an emergency, borrows heavily from the field of emergency planning known as *business resumption planning*, an activity which came into its own with private corporations in the late 1980s. The Emergency Program Coordinator will see common elements from areas such as business contingency planning, business continuation planning, business recovery planning and business disaster recovery planning. A selection of this material has been distilled into practical and prudent steps applicable to the public sector at the local government level.

The heavy dependence of [local governments] on technology and automated systems creates a vital need for [service continuation] plans[1]. In "The Disaster Recovery Planning Process" Wold notes that "[service continuation] planning involves more than off-site storage or back-up processing. [Local governments] should also develop written comprehensive [service continuation] plans that address all critical operations and functions ..."[2] Simply put, service continuation plans detail procedures to be followed after an emergency to facilitate the continuation of, or the expeditious recovery of, essential business functions. In this sense, such a plan can be viewed as pro-active rather than reactive, focussing on impact rather than cause.[3]

OBJECTIVES

The primary objective of a Service Continuation Plan is to protect the local government in the event that all or part of its service provision capability is impaired by an emergency. The timely implementation of such a plan should minimize the disruption of operations while ensuring that a focussed effort brings about an orderly recovery after an emergency.

THE PHYSICAL, HUMAN, TECHNOLOGY AND OPERATIONS MODEL

There are several aspects to service provision: facilities, people, records/data/information and systems (computers and telecommunications)[4]. The *Physical, Human, Technology, Operations (PHTO) Model* identifies the four essential elements in service delivery and provides the conceptual framework for the subsequent plan development. The following are examples of how each may be affected by an emergency:

a. Physical
   - town office destroyed/uninhabitable
   - files destroyed
   - office damaged by flood, fire, explosion, wind damage, prolonged power outage
   - Public Works office/yard unusable (impact on storage of vehicles/materials)

b. Human
   - manager(s) incapacitated
   - important systems operators incapacitated
     - Public Works functions (sewer treatment and water quality expertise)
     - computer hardware/software knowledge (accounting, fund allocation)

c. Technology
  - computer hardware/software breakdown
  - water/sewer provision fails
  - data files lost/destroyed/corrupted
  - temporary/permanent loss of data
  - telephone malfunction
  - radio system/Public Works alarm systems/SCADA systems fail

d. Operations
  - revenues to accounts
  - transfer of funds
  - withdrawal of funds
  - payment of bills (accounts payable)
  - issuance of bills and notices (accounts receivable)
  - continuance of Council (alternate meeting locations)
  - client needs
    - counter information
    - infrastructure services (roads/water/sewer)

These only represent a cursory attempt to enumerate possible impacts of each element. As the size of the local government grows, so too will the extent and complexity of the services and functions it provides. Each element of the *Physical, Human, Technology, Operations Model* then represents an increasingly precarious cornerstone in support of continued service provision.

MAXIMUM TOLERABLE DISRUPTION TIME

An important aspect of service continuation planning is prioritizing services. A number of methods are proposed in the literature and vary widely. This work will use a measure called *Maximum Tolerable Disruption Time (MTDT)* and is as follows:

Maximum Tolerable Disruption Time (MTDT)	Priority
< 1 to 1 day	1
2 to 4 days	2
5 to 7 days	3
8 to 10 days	4
> 10 days	5

This provides a simple scheme for prioritizing critical service functions while providing a quantitative measure of the potential impact of the loss of that service.

PLANNING TASKS

Again, the literature in this area is quite varied in terms of the actual steps in undertaking a service continuation planning exercise. The most logical of the many approaches has been proposed by Burns and is as follows in a slightly modified form:

**EIGHT STEPS OF
SERVICE CONTINUATION PLANNING**

1. Planning Scenarios and Assumptions
2. Service Impact Analysis (identify critical service functions)
3. Critical Service Function Priority Setting
4. Compiling the Plan
5. Emergency Program Planning Committee and Senior Management Endorsement
6. Communicate the Plan
7. Realistic Testing
8. Maintain the Plan[5]

These will each be addressed in more detail in the following section.

PLAN DEVELOPMENT

As with the general Emergency Management Plan and the hazard-specific preparedness plans, the Service Continuation Plan is prepared under the direction of the Emergency Program Planning Committee.

A team of specialists is required to develop a Service Continuation Plan. These will be experts in areas other than emergency planning so the Emergency Program Coordinator should act in the role of facilitator and chair this group. This group should include the heads of all major functional areas within the local government. This planning effort should be brought to the attention of all line managers in the local government, so not only are they aware of the development of such a plan, they are able to contribute ideas and alternatives to their representative on this planning team.

PLAN FOR THE WORST CASE SCENARIO

The initial step in developing the plan is to state the basic assumptions upon which it will be based. These assumptions will vary according to the size of the local government and whether it is a specialized local government, e.g. improvement area, fire protection district, etc. Assumptions could include the loss of computing capability, uninhabitable facilities, or loss of essential personnel. Anything that could have an impact on how, when, where and by whom the critical services will be delivered should be considered. In general terms, this is planning for the worst-case scenario and doing so should include natural, technical and human threats[6]. Lesser scenarios will be covered, ensuring the local government is prepared to recover from a range of possibilities.

SERVICE IMPACT ANALYSIS

A service impact analysis should cover all the service functions performed by the local government and determine which specific functions are essential to continued local government operations. These are known as *critical service functions.*

The following list of questions may assist in identifying critical service functions:
- What does the local government provide continuously? Can it be stopped or postponed? What do residents and other clients rely on the local government for?
- What external inputs does the local government need to continue to function? What if any of these stop?
- What are the immediate and ongoing internal requirements? Where/who do these come from?
- How long can we be without what?
- What are the regulatory requirements and penalties if a particular function is temporarily stopped or suspended?
- What is the financial impact of non-performance of one/some/all of these functions? What is the relative significance? Can it be measured?
- What is the cost of response/recovery actions for continued uninterrupted service versus short-term non-performance (penalties, inconvenience, etc.)?
- What legal or contractual liabilities would arise from the non-performance of a function?
- What are the public relations implications of a curtailment of one/some/all functions?
- What are the safety/security implications of interrupted service or non-performance?
- Which functions are computer-dependent, which have back-up systems and do staff know how to operate it? How long can it operate? What are

the implications of entering this manual information once the system is up and running again?

- Does the local government's Emergency Management Plan allow for the rotation of staff if prolonged operations are required?
- Is there an inventory of essential operating information and a checklist of essential records? Are copies of essential records maintained off-site?
- Has critical computer hardware and software been identified?
- What work-in-progress is underway and what would be the impact if it is lost?
- What work-in-progress elsewhere (as input into the local government) is being done and what would the damage be if lost?

In compiling the list of critical service functions, the needs of each functional area should be thoroughly evaluated in terms of key personnel, information, processing systems, service, documentation, vital records, and policies and procedures (see Appendix A1). A suitable framework for this task is the *Physical, Human, Technology, Operations Model* introduced earlier. This will assist in identifying all aspects of the four variables which may be weaknesses in continued service provision.

In considering critical service functions and those weaknesses identified by the *Physical, Human, Technology, Operations Model*, it is also necessary to list the resources and support required to perform these functions and the alternatives. These would include alternate staff, manual systems, off-site storage, backup processing and specific vendor-supplied resources on short notice.

Once the services provided by the local government have been enumerated and the critical service functions identified, a risk assessment must be conducted to assess the degree of exposure faced by each. This has more or less been completed in planning for the worst-case scenario where natural, technical and human threats have been anticipated, and the weaknesses in uninterrupted service provision identified by the *Physical, Human, Technology, Operations Model*. It is the impact of any exposure on continued service provision which needs to be balanced against the criticality of that particular function.

CRITICAL SERVICE FUNCTION PRIORITY SETTING

From the service impact analysis emerges a list of critical service functions and an idea of the degree of risk exposure for each. The next step is to prioritize the critical service functions using the *Maximum Tolerable Disruption Time* framework. From this a list will emerge ranking those functions on the spectrum from the service that simply cannot be interrupted, to those that can wait a number of days before service must be restored. Depending on the size of the local government or whether it is a special purpose government, the ranking of a number of services may vary widely.

For example, small communities in Canada may only have protective services (police and fire), water and sewer as the only priority one services while utility bills and dog licenses are not critical and can wait several days before being restored. A large metropolitan center, especially American cities which offer a much wider range of social services than Canadian cities, may have an extensive list of critical service functions and many ranking number one.

After a priority has been determined, the necessary step in transposing a priority service into an actionable plan is to develop a specific objective for each critical service function. The objective will balance the criticality of the service with the realities of the resources and support required to overcome the *Physical, Human, Technology, Operations Model*-identified weaknesses. Don't lose sight of the fact that the planning mindset here is the worst-case scenario. Lesser emergencies may not see any service disruption or be ones from which recovery is very straightforward. Therefore, for worst-case scenario planning, examples of service restoration could be the full provision of service "X" within three days after an emergency, whereas partial provision of service "X" within one day of the emergency with full service "X" provision within three days is an alternative. A sample standardized form for this exercise is included in Appendix A1.

When developing these objectives, Burbridge cautions against losing sight of the corporate objectives[7]. These objectives may be larger emergency management objectives, specific service continuation goals or generally applicable corporate customer service standards. Where these apply, they will provide some guidance to the development of service-specific objectives.

Tremendous time and effort will have been put into reviewing all services provided, determining the critical services, assessing their exposure to risk and prioritizing their importance. All of this work is for naught if well thought out and realistic planning objectives are not used to translate that work into practice. Sage advice from an early mentor still rings true: objectives must be simple, measurable and achievable.

COMPILING THE PLAN

The substance of the Service Continuation Plan comes from determining what resources and support are required to achieve those planning objectives for each critical service function. It is the compilation and organization of these procedures and resources that make the plan.

Resources would include arranging alternate computing centers or perhaps laptop computers, alternate work sites, stationery supplies for manually recording operations which are normally automated (this may include forms), alternates for key staff members who either manage or perform specific critical functions, telephones, alternate power supplies and short-notice supply of office machines such as fax, photocopier and adding machines.

Support would include flexible and short-notice provision of supplies, hardware, software and other consultant services that are normal inputs to the local government operation. Support also needs to come from the Chief Administrative Officer and Council for expenditure of the necessary funds to acquire the needed resources and support at the discretion of those key staff members.

Procedures would include an activation scheme for the Service Continuation Plan, a telephone list of key staff members and their alternates, a procedure for relocating to an alternate site, ensuring that manual systems still function and that specific staff members are trained and kept proficient on them. If manual systems are to be used as a means of getting a service operational again, establish a procedure for ensuring the manually handled information is entered into the primary system once that is functional again. This will take time and incur a cost which must be considered a corollary of using manual systems.

This is in no way an exhaustive listing of resources, support and procedures. It is indicative of the types of such that may be needed. As the steps detailed previously in the chapter on Plan Development are actually performed in the local government setting, the needs of each critical service function planning objective should become self-evident. They then need to be documented, usually in the form of an action checklist, and collated into a plan.

Service Continuation Plan Outline

Purpose
Annual Review
Scope
Concept of Operation
Objectives
Activation
Basic Assumptions
Service Impact Analysis
    Critical Service Functions
    Risk Assessment
    Critical Service Function Priorities and Objectives
Initial Response
    Alternate Processing Systems (Manual Systems)
    Alternate Site
    Immediate Action Checklists
    Back-up Computing
    Equipment Suppliers
Restoration of Service Level
    Entering Manual Records
    New Equipment
Appendices
    Suppliers' Contact Information
    Staff Contact Information (to include alternates)

SENIOR LEVEL ENDORSEMENT

Once a documented plan is produced, it should be presented to senior management for ratification. First, since the Emergency Program Coordinator and the service continuation planning team are preparing this plan under the auspices of the Emergency Program Planning Committee, the draft plan should be presented to this committee to ensure it is a thorough and professional emergency planning document and is consistent with the other initiatives under the broader *Comprehensive Emergency Management Plan*.

The Service Continuation Plan should then be presented to the Chief Administrative Officer and to the Mayor and Council for approval. This is different from the Emergency Management Plan and hazard-specific preparedness plans which are approved solely by the Emergency Program Planning Committee. In this latter case, the plans are putting in place a management framework and immediate action drills for response. The Chief Administrative Officer and his/her senior managers step into this framework and manage the emergency. The Service Continuation Plan is fundamentally different for it represents the very manner in which the direction and policies of Council will be executed, by definition, in a temporary, expeditious and less-refined manner. Acknowledgement of this must be made by the top officials for it to be confidently executed by the mangers and staff.

COMMUNICATE THE PLAN

Once the plan is in place, all staff must be made aware that such provisions have been made. Presumably, those department heads or key managers who will have major responsibilities when this plan is implemented have participated in its development. Now is the time to ensure that those designated alternates and all those involved in the particular service delivery streams are aware of what the procedure will be if normal operations are not possible. It is imperative that everyone likely to be involved in these alternate service delivery operations be aware of what may occur and how that service will be delivered.

Surprising staff with such plans as an emergency occurs will cause confusion and do harm to the organizational cohesiveness, required to be that much more resilient under such times of stress. When ascertaining who to make aware of these plans, cast the net wider than one might first determine because alternate key staff members may be the third, fourth or fifth down the list. Depending on how large the organization is, it maybe prudent to educate the all staff members on what is being planned for, and how alternative service delivery will be carried out.

EXERCISE AND EVALUATION

No confidence can be put in any emergency plan unless it has been thoroughly tested. This is especially true for service continuation plans. Such a plan represents the very basic functioning of a local government as it recovers from a major emergency. For confidence to be invested in such a plan, a complete and thorough exercise and evaluation scheme must be completed.

Exercising the plan provides the local government with a degree of confidence that all necessary elements have been included. Other reasons for testing include:
- determining the feasibility and compatibility of backup facilities and procedures;
- identifying areas in the plan that need modification;
- providing training to the team managers and team members;
- demonstrating the ability of the organization to recover; and,

- providing motivation for maintaining and updating the Service Continuation Plan[8].

Wold identifies four types of Service Continuation Plan exercises: checklists, simulation, parallel tests and full interruption tests. Further, he notes a test of the plan should be performed by conducting a structured walk-through test. The test will provide additional information regarding any further steps that may need to be included, changes in procedures that are not effective, and other appropriate adjustments[9].

MAINTENANCE AND UPDATING

After such initial testing refines the plan, a program of annual review and exercise should be maintained at the direction of the Emergency Program Planning Committee. Since this plan is both fundamental to the emergency operation and recovery of the local government, and the fact that the plan is based on key personnel, specific systems and detailed procedures, any significant change to personnel, systems, procedures and internal/external supply and provision arrangements must be reflected in the plan with amendments done as those organizational changes are made. The annual review not only reviews the plan for continued relevance, but also reviews those organizational changes that have been made to ensure the planning objectives for each critical service function are still being met.

FACILITIES

Different types of emergencies will have different effects on the facilities of, and within, the local government. For example, floods may undermine foundations while an explosion may stove in walls and windows, and an earthquake may inflict serious structural damage. Also, not only will the local government be called upon to assess their facilities for structural integrity and continued habitability, it will also be called on to do so for other "community" structures such as hospitals and schools.

With seismic retrofitting of buildings and flood control measures being notable exceptions, little else can be done to prepare an otherwise sound structure for a range of unknown emergencies. Local governments can, however, prepare ahead of time for the task of inspecting buildings after an emergency has occurred by adopting a type of triage for buildings and applying this to a hierarchy of prioritized facilities.

Some local governments may wish to formalize these steps into a plan such as follows.

Facilities Inspection and Repair Plan

Purpose
Annual Review
Scope
Concept of Operation
Objectives
Activation
Deemed Qualified Professionals
Post-Emergency Evaluation
    Rapid Evaluation
    Detailed Evaluation
    Engineering Evaluation
Post-Inspection Classification
    Inspected
    Limited Entry
    Unsafe
Non-Structural Hazards
Essential Facilities
    Designated
    Facility Plans
    Designated Inspectors
    Pre-Emergency Inspection and Familiarization
Repair Planning
    Fixed Equipment Inventory
Appendices
    Contact Information and Alternates
    Inspectors
    Major Equipment Suppliers
    Specialty Resources

POST-EMERGENCY STRUCTURAL ANALYSIS

The local government building inspection function will be taxed by the requests for safety inspections in the immediate post-emergency period, assuming an emergency has occurred that is capable of damaging structures. Depending on the size and population density of the jurisdiction, the nature and extent of the emergency, and the degree of vertical build-up in the urban area, the amount of work will vary from manageable to overwhelming. Even with the assistance of outside support and trained volunteers, trained staff may be in short supply so an effective system of being able to triage damaged buildings is necessary.

California's Applied Technology Council, in its publication <u>Procedures for Post-Earthquake Safety Evaluations of Buildings</u>, advocates a very useful three-level system of post-emergency building evaluation. It consists of initially a rapid evaluation, a detailed evaluation and finally a full structural engineering evaluation. Each level also involves marking the structure as to the result of the evaluation with standardized placards indicating that the structure has been inspected and is either subject to entry or is unsafe.

Most large-scale emergencies will have an identifiable area which has been the most greatly affected. This is the hardest hit area and could be ground zero of an explosion, the epicenter of an earthquake or the path of a tornado. Radiating out from this area either concentrically from an omni-directional blast or an earthquake, in a lobe if a directional blast, or parallel to the path of a linear event, will be areas of decreasing damage. Given the nature of the generally overwhelming task of inspection, it is logical to start with the hardest hit area first. As structures and facilities in this area are dealt with the inspection effort can move progressively into less affected areas with buildings and facilities not as heavily damaged.

Rapid inspection of buildings should occur within the first few hours or days of an emergency (when safe to do so considering aftershocks, gas leaks, fire, etc.) and can be conducted by individuals the local building inspection department deems qualified. This evaluation is based on a very general external examination of the building looking at certain structural elements, obvious deformations or departures from the intended appearance that are indicative of serious safety concerns. At this very early point in the recovery process speed is of the essence in order to conduct this preliminary safety assessment in order to avoid the public returning to unsafe buildings.

After a rapid evaluation has been completed and the appropriate professionals are available, the detailed evaluations can take place. These can occur any time in the first few hours or days after an emergency and after the rapid evaluations have occurred. Detailed evaluations are to be conducted by Structural Engineers and are based on visual observations but involving a much more thorough examination of the building. This will involve examining structural elements, such as frames, walls and the vertical and lateral load-bearing members. The objective here is to determine whether a building or facility can return to service before repairs are made.

The third and final stage is the full engineering evaluation. Whereas the rapid and detailed evaluations are considered part of the local government coordinated recovery effort, this evaluation is conducted by a consulting Structural Engineer retained by the building or facility owner. Obviously, local governments will act in the capacity of owner for public buildings and facilities but private property owners are responsible for their own engineering evaluation. This evaluation commences as soon as possible which is expected to be several days after the emergency. It is a thorough examination that may take up to a week and involves destructive testing, review of construction drawings and new structural calculations which results in a repair plan for that building. The objective is to return the building to as near new as possible.

 These three levels of evaluation are detailed in the following table[10].

BUILDING EVALUATION TECHNIQUES			
Technique	Required Personnel	Goal	Time/Building
Rapid Evaluation	Qualified building inspectors, Civil/Structural Engineers, Architects, other individuals deemed qualified by the local jurisdiction	Rapid assessment of safety. Used to quickly post obviously unsafe and apparently safe structures, and to identify buildings requiring Detailed Evaluation	10-20 minutes
Detailed Evaluation	Structural Engineer	damaged buildings and questionable situations. Used to identify buildings requiring an Engineering Evaluation	1-4 hours
Engineering Evaluation	Consulting Structural Engineer	Detailed engineering evaluation of damaged buildings, involving use of construction drawings, damage data, and new structural calculations	1-7 days or more

Once evaluation of the building has taken place it should be placarded to indicate the degree of danger posed. The following table summarizes these levels[11].

BUILDING SAFETY EVALUATION CLASSIFICATIONS		
Posting Classification	Colour	Description
Inspected	Green	No apparent hazard found, although repairs may be required. Original lateral load capacity not significantly decreased. No restriction on use or occupancy.
Limited Entry	Yellow	Dangerous condition believed to be present. Entry by owner permitted only for emergency purposes and only at own risk. No usage on continuous basis. Entry by public not permitted. Possible major aftershock hazard.
Unsafe	Red	Extreme hazard, may collapse. Imminent danger of collapse from an aftershock. Unsafe for occupancy or entry, except by authorities.

Two additional aspects to consider in the post-emergency building and facility evaluation are *geotechnical* and *non-structural* hazards.

Geotechnical hazards involve ground movements, either during or after the emergency. Such hazards can be static where the movement has already occurred or is poised to occur, or dynamic indicating continuous movement such as mud or settling of disturbed material. The results of this hazard can be surface fault rupture resulting in both horizontal and vertical ground movement, slope failure resulting in an undermined foundation or stresses due to differential pressures, other differential ground movements such as liquefaction, and, finally, earth dam or reservoir movement resulting in compromised integrity. Where these are present or suspected, a Geotechnical Engineer should be involved.

Finally, **non-structural elements** should be assessed for additional or ongoing hazards. Generally this involves securing an affected area where there is a falling debris hazard. This may include parapets, canopies, external fixtures and glazing. Other non-structural elements posing a safety hazard are curtain walls, ceiling and elevated fixtures, mechanical and electrical fixtures, and elevators. These should be assessed by the appropriate professional and should be cordoned off until deemed safe.

ESSENTIAL FACILITIES

Essential facilities deserve special attention in the planning stages to ensure rapid recovery and return to service. Such facilities may include hospitals, health care facilities, police and fire stations, jails and detention centers, communications centers, and Emergency Operations Centers[12]. Prioritizing essential facilities and having designated inspection officials with relevant drawings, plans and studies available will ease the task of inspection. It is considered wise to have these designated inspectors tour the facility in anticipation of an emergency to become familiar with all aspects of the building and grounds. In addition to these two components, fixed equipment should be noted and consideration given to the type of expertise required to restore that function. Fixed equipment would include main boilers, chillers, emergency generators, fuel tanks, battery racks, fire pumps, on-site water storage, communications equipment, main transformers, main electrical panels, and elevators[13]. Such preparations will ensure that essential facilities will get prompt evaluation following an emergency and that critical fixed equipment will be quickly restored. Ensuring the safety and integrity of essential facilities will ease the recovery function.

REPAIR AND REBUILDING

Once full engineering evaluations are completed, building owners will want to commence repair and rebuilding efforts. This will require permits, approval and inspections from the local building inspection department which has already performed a yeoman service in the rapid evaluation of buildings. The local jurisdiction is responsible for the enforcement of the building code which will need to be adhered to in reconstruction activities. It is highly probable that additional staff may be needed to process permits, review plans and inspect work in such a major rebuilding endeavor. It may be necessary to employ professionals such as Architects and Engineers to assist staff in meeting this demand. Ultimately, staff can only process and inspect work at a human pace so the type of work submitted may have to be prioritized, e.g., demolitions, unsafe buildings, cosmetic repairs, high priority buildings, etc. This may then allow a logical progression to the rebuilding activities.

TIMEFRAME

Potentially, the restoration of buildings and facilities may be a protracted affair lasting many months. Not only may civic and other buildings and facilities be out of commission for some time, the physical operation of the jurisdiction may be somewhat impaired with the clearing of debris, demolition of buildings, and streets and sidewalks occupied with heavy equipment involved in rebuilding. It must be recognized that, potentially, the recovery phase could take some time to pass depending ultimately on the nature of the emergency, the density of the population, and the scale of urbanization.

STAFF

Local government employees may be affected by an emergency in very personal ways. The person will be affected first as an individual, then as a family member, as an employee and finally as a member of a community.

As an individual the person may have been physically injured or mentally traumatized by a personal near miss or the destruction from the event. As a family member all of the person's thoughts and energy will be directed at ensuring their safety and comfort: other family members may have been injured, may be missing or the family residence may have suffered damage. As an employee, normal duties will yield to emergency duties which involve handling or assessing information on the degree of injury and damage. The local government response function must rapidly collect and analyze information.

Staff members are not accustomed to such unappealing tasks and this will take a toll on physical and mental stamina. Finally, as a member of the community at large, the sense of loss and hopelessness in the face of widespread severe injury and damage will affect all those who lived, worked and shopped in the community. Human beings are not automatons and cannot be expected to experience an emergency at these multiple levels without being affected to some extent. The local government planning a response to, and recovery from, a large-scale emergency must understand and anticipate this human element.

While it is difficult and often impractical to prepare staff members for the types of impact they may experience after an emergency, the organization must prepare for these results. *Critical Incident Stress Debriefing* is an effective approach to post-emergency personal recovery for municipal staff.

CRITICAL INCIDENT STRESS DEBRIEFING

Critical Incident Stress is defined as:

> *"Any situation faced by an emergency service personnel that causes them to experience unusually strong emotional reactions which have the potential to interfere with their ability at the scene or later … all that is necessary is that the incident, regardless of type, generates unusually strong feelings in the emergency service worker.[14]"*

While originally designed for use with traditional emergency services personnel, in recent years Critical Incident Stress Debriefing has gained a wider scope of application to now include any persons adversely traumatized by involvement in an emergency including responders, support staff, witnesses, and victims.

The purpose of Critical Incident Stress Debriefing is to:
- lessen the impact of major events on emergency services personnel; and,
- accelerate normal recovery in normal people who are experiencing normal stress after experiencing highly abnormal events or incidents.

An actual debriefing is a meeting of those affected by what they encounter as an emergency occurs, is responded to, or is recovered from. It is facilitated by an individual or team of professional counsellors trained in handling these types of reactions.

As the name implies, the feelings those affected encounter are due to stress. Critical Incident Stress Debriefing recognizes the need to deal with this stress which is accomplished by allowing those affected to talk about their experience, their feelings and their subsequent reactions due to those feelings. The meetings, which may vary in the number of participants, provide a comfortable and supportive environment for people to discuss their feelings as well as to ensure they know that such reactions are perfectly normal. One of the most important aspects of these sessions is that it imparts on the individual coping techniques for dealing with their emotions in the days, weeks and months following the emergency so as to assist them in keeping the emergency and their role in it in proper perspective.

It is imperative that such debriefing sessions occur as soon as possible, if not immediately as staff are relieved from duty, so as to provide the persons involved with the opportunity to share experiences and feelings so they are assured they have no need to carry adverse feelings or regrets about their roles. Delays in getting this assistance allows various negative reactions to the stress to take hold in the individual and becoming increasingly difficult to dislodge or rectify.

Not every emergency will necessitate the use of Critical Incident Stress Debriefing. However, in anticipation of a major emergency with the levels of destruction, injury and death which requires this type of support, properly trained counsellors should be identified as a resource to be called upon when needed.

Minimum Service Levels

While this topic has been touched upon under Service Continuation Planning, it must be considered from the staffing perspective. After a major emergency staff may be unable to perform their assigned duties due to injury, psychological trauma, or the need to attend to family matters. This then necessitates the local government to assess the recovery phase from the perspective of how few people are critical to continued minimum operations levels. While this is tied closely to the analysis conducted under service continuation planning, meeting those identified commitments and service levels may in fact require the use of staff not normally assigned to a specific department, or other comparably trained professionals as substitutes.

Rest and Recovery Period

As already mentioned, the recovery phase may take weeks, months or even years. The intensity of emergency operations should wind down dramatically in the short-term following a major emergency while the mid- to long-term will require a more protracted approach.

Humans have a capacity to perform at above average levels for various lengths of time but not indefinitely. Thus, even with proper shift rotation, the intense immediate response can only be sustained for a short period of perhaps several days as a maximum before rest and recovery are necessary to prevent physical and mental burnout. After the intensity of initial response, the longer-term management of the recovery phase, while less intense than the "all-out" response, still requires above-average contribution by participants. Participants may be able to sustain these levels for longer periods, perhaps a week or two or three depending on the task performed, before a rest and recovery period.

The rest and recovery period is a real aspect of the recovery phase which the Emergency Program Coordinator must encompass. Rest and recovery is not tokenism either. Individuals must be allowed a sufficient period to physically and mentally recover. This is facilitated much more rapidly if the person can leave the affected area.

This section is not advocating a responsibility on the local government to provide the actual rest and recovery transportation and destination. Ultimately this is up to the individual. It behoves the Emergency Program Coordinator to be aware of this aspect of the recovery phase and to allow for it to occur when determining recovery timetables and scheduling relief shift work.

EQUIPMENT AND SUPPLIES

Part of the recovery process is eventually getting all equipment fully operational again and returning supplies of various materials destroyed or consumed back to normal operational levels. Critical elements of equipment and supplies have been addressed under *Service Continuation Planning*. This section is intended to briefly highlight the need, at some point as the emergency winds down, to consider repairs to equipment and the re-supply of various materials and items.

Depending on the scope of the emergency, the speed with which repairs and re-supply may be procured will vary. In a regional-scale emergency, delays may be lengthy as limited resources are quickly utilized. Skilled technicians required for repair may be scheduled for several weeks or months while various re-supply requests may have to come from out of region/county, province/state or country. Smaller scale emergencies may experience faster recovery due to the greater availability of technicians and supplies required.

To be thorough, the types of technicians and material suppliers may be kept current in a resource list for ease of reference. However, in the overall scope of the emergency and its recovery, these are not critical elements nor is there response pressures to demand immediate results. While it is important that repair and re-supply occur as expeditiously as possible, time is usually available for the various affected responsible departments to organize this on their own accord.

The complete and thorough Emergency Program Coordinator will anticipate some of these needs when also planning for maintenance of critical functions. However, it is difficult, especially in a large local government, to have a realistic grasp on the full span of repair and re-supply for each department. The important point is that this part of the recovery process is recognized by the Emergency Program Coordinator as one aspect which dictates the speed of complete and final recovery.

EMERGENCY OPERATIONS CENTER

The general purpose of the Emergency Operations Center is to provide support to the site and coordination of the overall operation (evacuation, reception centers, public information and recovery). To do this it needs to be staffed by those whose expertise is needed. As that expertise is no longer required that aspect of the Emergency Operations Center shuts down. This transition is indicative of the shift from "*Response* Emergency Operations Center" to "*Recovery* Emergency Operations Center."

The "Response Emergency Operations Center" in a major emergency will see a wide range of members in addition to the response services. Once the actual emergency has passed and these response services begin their own internal recovery operations, the membership of the Emergency Operations Center lessens to those required to support and coordinate recovery operations such as public health, public works, engineering, emergency social services, etc. These are the longer-term aspects of recovery which may stretch from weeks to months. At some point in this transition, the nature of the support and coordination problems become less urgent and become simply "management" type of problems. While they will still require the coordination efforts of many agencies, there is no need for staffing the Emergency Operations Center around the clock.

Eventually the Emergency Operations Center becomes a "regular work hours" meeting of these agencies which is sustainable indefinitely, in theory. However, at some point the "response" aspect of engineering/public works issues moves into the regular, albeit now modified, capital works program while, eventually, the last people leave emergency shelters to stay with other family members or into new living arrangements. At this point the Emergency Operations Center ceases to have a purpose to exist.

The wind-up of an Emergency Operations Center is a very poorly defined time. Many elements specific to the event, location and the persons involved will determine how and when this occurs. Coordination and support are the essential elements, and when these are no longer required the termination is at hand. Conversely, prematurely shutting down the Emergency Operations Center may prolong recovery if cooperation between agencies is hindered through lack of coordination.

The actual shut down of the Emergency Operations Center is a critical time for the Emergency Program Coordinator. Service logs must be collected and master event logs preserved. Such documents, and any others recording the decision-making process, will form the legal and historical record for any possible legal action which may follow. Depending on whether or not the Emergency Operations Center is a permanent fixture at City Hall, various aspects of telecommunications may need to be disconnected and stored for future use, allowing the room to return to its normal use.

If it is a permanent, ready to use facility, all aspects of the Center must be readied once again for future use. This may involve replacing maps and equipment consumed in the process and repairing or replacing faulty equipment. When time permits, preferably shortly after the Emergency Operations Center has been deactivated, convene a meeting of the participants for a debriefing with respect to operations and equipment in the Emergency Operations Center. Any use of the Emergency Operations Center, whether on exercise or an actual emergency, provides a great opportunity to learn how and where to improve the operation for the next time.

RETURNING TO NORMAL: WHEN DOES THE RECOVERY PERIOD END?

Some experts assert that a community never returns to normal after a major emergency. Depending upon the severity of the emergency, certain buildings may not be rebuilt or the reconstruction may take on a new look by providing an opportunity to redo things according to a new plan. Also, businesses slow in their recovery stand a poor chance of re-opening their doors, thereby introducing a new social dynamic into a neighbourhood or community that is recovering.

These elements largely have a psychological impact as in the post-emergency period people remain on edge anticipating the next emergency or adjust to the reconstruction which is simply different from that which existed before the emergency. From a physical rebuilding perspective, recovery operations can generally be considered complete when the impact of the emergency, such as toppled buildings, broken infrastructure, etc., are removed and individual property owners can then consider their rehabilitation options. True, demolition, reconstruction, and other activities will continue at the discretion of the respective property owners, but these activities occur daily in an urban community, granted for other, largely economic reasons, rather than due to an emergency.

When viewed from the local government perspective, an end to the emergency must be determined, even if arbitrarily, for legal and other liability reasons, as well as for avoiding inclusion of the lengthy process where property owners make private property decisions as to their personal best options. A local government must consider the recovery period finished when its infrastructure is fully operational at pre-emergency levels and not operating on any temporary or makeshift arrangements. Depending on the extent of the damage, such as toppled elevated roads and massive water and sewer damage, this "local government" recovery may be very protracted but must end when the public interest has been served.

Therefore, it is possible to define an end to the recovery phase from a local government perspective. However, it may not necessarily be returning to the "normal" of the pre-emergency period but can be considered a "post-emergency normal" where the destruction allows for better layout and servicing considerations. This "post-emergency normal" is restoring the local government and its services to a normal operating mode albeit, hopefully, in a new and better manner.

Finally, the question is often asked whether the local government will ever recover as an organization. It can be said that the organization will recover but it may not be the same: possibly not the same in terms of operational flexibility, service delivery, physical structure and organizational culture. It is extremely difficult and rare to go through a major, or even moderate, emergency without learning something which affects the "who, what, where, when and how" of local government operations. While the local government will get past the particular emergency, it will be slightly different for having experienced the emergency. Sometimes almost imperceptible, sometimes radical, the extent of impact and subsequent organizational change depends on the degree of exposure the local government has with emergencies.

Key Points

- The issue of when does recovery start
- Service Continuation plans for the worst-case scenario
- Service Continuation Plans are implemented immediately upon identifying a critical service delivery being adversely affected
- PHTO Model for identifying vulnerable service delivery elements
- MTDT framework assists in prioritizing critical service functions
- Eight step process for Service Continuation Planning
- Public facilities susceptible to damage require post-emergency structural analysis with a priority on critical facilities
- Three level assessment of increasing detail for facility evaluation

- After evaluation, building placards with a three color system indicate degree of habitability
- The human element of service delivery in the post-emergency phase requires attention to ensure the ability to perform critical functions
- Critical Incident Stress Debriefing is a controlled process where witnesses can discuss the emergency with the intent of lessening the impact and accelerating personal recovery
- Incorporate minimum service levels and rest and recovery periods into recovery planning
- While recovery of the community at large may take years, local government must consider the event over once damage to its service delivery mechanisms is repaired

---

[1] Wold, G.H., and Shriver, R.F. 1993. *Selecting Business Recovery Strategies*. Disaster Recovery Journal. Jul/Aug/Sep.

[2] Wold, G.H. 1992. *The Disaster Recovery Planning Process*. Disaster Recovery Journal. Jan/Feb/Mar.

[3] Modified from the unpublished 1992 B.C. Ministry of Finance and Corporate Relations manual *Business Continuation Planning*.

[4] *ibid.*

[5] Burns, E. 1994. *Surviving a Disaster Takes a Plan, Not a Miracle!* Disaster Recovery Journal. Jul/Aug/Sep.

[6] Wold, G.H. 1992. *supra.*

[7] Burbridge, J. 1989. *Is Your Organization Ready For A Disaster?* Emergency Preparedness Digest. Jul-Sep.

[8] Wold, G.H. 1992. *supra.*

[9] *ibid.*

[10] Taken from <u>Procedures for Post-Earthquake Safety Evaluation of Buildings</u>, Applied Technology Council, 1989.

[11] *ibid.*

[12] *ibid.*

[13] *ibid.*

[14] "When Disaster Strikes... The Critical Incident Stress Debriefing Process" by Jeffery Mitchell in *Journal of Emergency Medical Services*. Vol. 8, 1983.

5

PUTTING IT ALL TOGETHER

> The assembly of a Comprehensive Emergency Management Plan is not the end of the process: it is merely the first step. Equally important elements of overall preparedness include educating staff and the general public, training staff and volunteers, conducting realistic exercises and the ongoing monitoring and revising of the entire plan..

...AND KEEPING IT ALL TOGETHER

The major chapters of this book have focused on the four components of *Comprehensive Emergency Management*: mitigation, preparedness, response and recovery. This conceptual framework is the backbone of good emergency planning for any organization, even beyond local governments. This process sees the development of a Comprehensive Emergency Management Plan from hazard identification, through plan development, to post-emergency assessment and wrap-up as conveyed in the following illustration.

COMPREHENSIVE EMERGENCY MANAGEMENT						
MITIGATION	+	PREPAREDNESS	+	RESPONSE	+	RECOVERY
Hazard Identification		Emergency Management		ICS if Multiple Jurisdictions		Service Continuation Plan
Hazard Assessment		Hazard-Specific Preparedness Plans		Mutual Aid Agreements		Facility Assessment and Repair
Mitigation Efforts and Risk Management		Exercise Schedule (different types over multiple years)		Resource Lists		Staff Debriefing
		Annual Review		State of Local Emergency		EOC Wrap-up
				County/ State/ Provincial State of Emergency		
				Public Information		

On the surface, this largely academic exercise seems to arrive at a point where a degree of comfort and reliance can be invested in the work undertaken. Conceivably, and unfortunately all too often, such work then is placed on the shelf only to be called upon when an emergency befalls the local government. Questions then arise such as who is responsible for this plan, who recalls its contents, what actions do we take, which people are required, what resources are required and who has those resources? When an emergency occurs, especially where the plan is held in reserve for "the big one," then at the very least a costly delay, if not confusion, will occur. This delay will defeat one of the primary tenets of such planning: smooth, efficient, immediate and nearly automatic actions to facilitate a rapid response in the face of human nature – which tends towards slow reactions.

Throughout this work it has been stressed that the general scope of applicability for the overall Comprehensive Emergency Management Plan, or certainly sub-plans within it, includes everything from "routine" emergencies which are just marginally above the day-to-day activities of the traditional emergency response agencies where either that extra degree of coordination or those additional resources are required, to the true catastrophes. This somewhat frequent use or reliance on the plan, or parts thereof, is one way of ensuring some degree of familiarly with it by those who rely on it.

```
Comprehensive Emergency Management Plan

A. Mitigation
B. Preparedness Plan
    1.  Emergency Management Plan
    2.  Priority Common Plans
        i.    Emergency Public Information Plan
        ii.   Emergency Social Services Plan
        iii.  Evacuation Plan
        iv.   Emergency Telecommunications Plan
    3.  Hazard-Specific Preparedness Plans
C. Recovery Plan
    1.  Service Continuation Plan
    2.  Facilities Repair and Inspection Plan
```

Beyond this actual employment of the plan, a more structured means of imparting an understanding and awareness of emergency planning is critical. Many experts state that the actual plan development aspect is only 20% of the overall preparedness program; education being 30% and exercises being 50%. Unfortunately, most local governments consider the job done once the plan is written. This is a dangerous misconception. Until education and general awareness is heightened among both local government staff and the general public, a training program for key personnel is developed, and a multiple-year schedule of exercises of increasing complexity is developed, no local government should consider themselves fully prepared. An axiom to remember is, *never rely on a plan until it has been exercised*.

EDUCATION

General awareness of potential emergencies that may befall a community is knowledge every resident should possess. Unfortunately, in a busy modern life not everyone cares or has the time to fully inform himself or herself, instead making a dangerous miscalculation that some "system" will look after them. This places additional burden on the local government emergency program and a significant drain on resources and volunteers. Depending upon the nature, frequency and severity of potential emergencies threatening a particular local government jurisdiction, efforts in this area may take on an enhanced degree of urgency. Regardless, a public information campaign to heighten general public awareness is a wise pre-emptive measure by a local government as it encourages residents to consider their personal and family vulnerabilities, may prompt some to enhance their personal self-sufficiency – but most importantly, imparts upon them how the local government is prepared to respond to certain types of emergencies, what its capabilities are, how it will inform and move residents as needed, and what type of basic conditions they can expect should they need to rely on the emergency social services system.

Local government employees should be models for such personal and family preparedness and held to a higher degree of preparedness. They must ensure they and their own families are prepared. These employees must report for their designated emergency duties (assuming they have roles in such a case) and then focus on executing their tasks. Their actions are key to ensuring success of the overall Comprehensive Emergency Management Plan upon which so many more residents are relying for support and relief.

The nature of such a public education campaign need not be elaborate, costly or time-consuming. The actual message to be passed along needs to be clearly identified by the Emergency Program Planning Committee. This then can be made into a pamphlet, newspaper advertisement or television commercial. Pamphlets are the best medium as they can be left in many locations for pick up or actively distributed in target neighborhoods by emergency program volunteers or postal mail. Generally, the type of information to be included would be the nature, frequency, severity and area affected by certain types of emergencies; what the local government is doing *vis a vis* planning and mitigation; and, finally, guidelines for family preparedness, such as what type of supplies are required and for what period, e.g. 72 hours, they should be prepared to be self-sufficient. Local government employees can be reached through distributing such pamphlets with pay records, tax documents or any other regular mail out. The added importance of emergency preparedness should be stressed.

TRAINING

It should be acknowledged that not everyone who will be involved with developing and exercising the Comprehensive Emergency Management Plan will be fully versed in emergency management. Certainly the process will involve those professionals from the traditional emergency response agencies and will also attract those volunteers with an interest in emergency matters. However, others will be involved by virtue of their position, such as the Directors of Public Works and Leisure Services; or, willingness to volunteer time to the community, generally emergency social services volunteers and Amateur Radio operators. To gain the maximum benefit from everyone involved in this process, training must be recognized as fundamental to the program's success and should be provided as appropriate to all levels of the emergency program structure.

Training is a cornerstone in effective emergency management and can be generally divided into two categories: *planning* and *operations*. Of the two general types of training, planning would consist of courses in:

- hazard identification and risk assessment;
- mitigation techniques;
- plan construction and drafting;
- community emergency social services assessment;
- telecommunications planning;
- public information/media relations;
- volunteer recruitment;
- procuring community resources; and, exercise development.

Operations training would include:

- the Incident Command System;
- Emergency Operations Center operations;
- site command;
- reception center operations;
- evacuee registration and inquiry;
- radio message handling; and,
- agency-specific training such as casualty triage and hazardous materials.

Usually, the best way to organize who in the organization needs what type of training is to develop a training matrix (see sample in Appendix A2). This matrix will list the training that is available on the horizontal axis and the positions within the emergency program on the vertical axis. The Emergency Program Planning Committee should be the body that makes the decision on who needs what level of training since its membership includes that cross-section of key emergency management personnel from within the community. This will then provide a multiple-year guide for the training of the organization and directing individuals towards being fully trained in order to successfully accomplish their designated task.

Training is a commitment the local government must recognize and embrace. Sufficient resources need to be made available to the Emergency Program Planning Committee in order to achieve the objective of properly training its staff and volunteers. All too often, local governments are reluctant to invest valuable training budget dollars in volunteers. This is understandable given the transient nature of some volunteers but this reluctance needs to be overcome to ensure a well-rounded and properly trained emergency management organization.

EXERCISING THE PLAN

Every Emergency Program Coordinator should adopt the mantra, *never rely on a plan that has not been exercised*. Exercising a plan serves many purposes which all assist in refining it to the point where it is relevant and reliable. It has been said that exercising an emergency plan is 50% of the effort in creating a plan (20% planning, 30% training). It certainly can be the most difficult and time-consuming part of creating the plan, but it is not the end of the process. Creating an emergency plan is a cycle which involves writing the plan; providing the required training; exercising the plan; evaluating the results from the exercise; and, following up to ensure that problems or shortcomings are addressed. The process then repeats itself with changes to the written plan, any additional training as acquired, re-exercised, evaluated and followed up. This should be part of a multiple-year cycle of exercises in conjunction with the ongoing training of staff and volunteers, and the annual review of the plan and its sub-components.

So why exercise? An exercise puts the plan to a practical test which will either prove the plan to be flawless in meeting the needs of the community, which is rare, or will identify the weaknesses, inaccuracies or incorrect assumptions in the plan when put into practice. These are valuable lessons the community wants to be made aware of before the plan is called upon in a real emergency where lives may be at stake. An exercise, therefore, is defined as an activity designed to:

- promote emergency preparedness;
- test or evaluate emergency operations, policies, plans, procedures of facilities; and,
- train personnel in emergency management duties and to demonstrate operational capability[1].

However, the following caveat is noted: "Exercises consist of the performance of duties, tasks or operations very similar to the way they would be performed in a real emergency. However, the exercise performance is in response to a simulated event. Therefore, exercises require input to emergency personnel that motivates a realistic action."[2]

Lawson notes fourteen objectives of exercises:

- train employees in their emergency duties;
- increase employee awareness;
- improve individual performance;
- develop enthusiasm, knowledge, skills and a willingness to participate in emergencies;
- validate standard operating procedures;
- identify resource requirements;
- reveal resource and supply chain gaps;
- reveal planning weaknesses;
- identify requirements for mutual aid agreements;
- clarify roles and responsibilities;
- improve communications and coordination;
- demonstrate operational capability;
- test equipment; and,
- promote emergency preparedness.[3]

A complete exercise program typically consists of five types of exercises: *orientation seminar, drill, tabletop exercise, functional exercise* and *full-scale exercise*. These represent a steady progression towards the final full-scale test with the philosophy being that increasingly more significant problems may become known as the scale and scope of the exercises increase. These points can be rectified before the next exercise where it can be reviewed for appropriateness and then allowing attention to focussed on new issues. Each type of exercise is briefly reviewed[4]:

Orientation Seminar
- used to introduce or refresh participants to plans and procedures
- lecture, panel discussion, media presentations or talk throughs
- can involve all levels of personnel
- review of past cases for lessons learned
- *advantages*:
  - little or no cost
  - modest time commitment
  - quick method to brief persons or organizations on who are not involved on a daily basis
- *disadvantages*:
  - only covers broad topics

Drill
- tests a single emergency response function
  - involves actual field response
  - effectiveness lies in the focus on a single or relatively limited portion of the overall response system in order to evaluate and improve it
  - *advantages*:
  - allows for a single system to be isolated and analyzed in-depth
    - increases realism over tabletop exercises
    - modest commitment in terms of time, cost and resources
    - easiest exercise to design
    - provides response personnel with hands-on training and equipment use
  - *disadvantages*:
    - does not test integrated systems capabilities
    - difficult to overload system
    - provides capability to evaluate only a segment of the response system

Tabletop Exercise

- actions taken and discussion based on a described emergency situation plus a series of messages to the players
- practice problem solving for emergency situation
- ongoing discussion and critique of appropriateness of actions taken and decisions made
- participants practice a coordinated, effective response
- permits breaks before new messages delivered to discuss proper response
- will involve policy and/or coordination personnel
- *advantages*:
  - modest commitment in terms of time, cost and resources
  - effective method of reviewing plans, implementing procedures and policies
  - educational device to acquaint key public-private sector personnel with emergency responsibilities and procedures
  - acquaints emergency response personnel with each other on a personal basis
- *disadvantages*:
  - does not provide true test of the system's capabilities
  - provides superficial exercise of plans, procedures and staff capabilities
  - difficult to demonstrate system overload

Functional Exercise

- simulation of an emergency that includes a description of the situation, a timed sequence of messages, and communication between players and simulators
- EOC members practice a coordinated, effective response in a time-pressured, realistic emergency simulation
- individual and system performance is evaluated
- will involve policy and coordination personnel
- *advantages*:
  - increased realism over tabletop exercises
  - has ability to test integrated response of entire emergency management system
  - modest commitment in terms of time, cost and resources
- *disadvantages*:
  - scenario development can be difficult
  - can be difficult to acquire telephones, radio and television equipment to enhance realism

Full-Scale Exercise

- adds a field component that interacts with a functional exercise through simulated messages
- tests the deployment of seldom used resources
- will involve policy, coordination, operations and field personnel
- *advantages*:
  - less simulations, increased realism and greater stress
  - greater opportunity to evaluate integrated communication capability
  - ability to evaluate mobilization of resources and first responder capability
- *disadvantages*:
  - additional cost
  - greater chance of losing communication containment
  - increasing chance of mistaking exercise for actual emergency
  - additional emphasis placed on safety as a result of movement by first responder apparatus
  - requires time commitment and level of expertise to properly implement

The development of any of the above exercises generally follows a five-step process[5].

Step one is considered *Getting Started*. This involves assessing the capability to conduct an exercise, defining its scope, selecting the type of exercise, addressing the costs and liabilities, and announcing the exercise.

Step two, *Exercise Development*, involves identifying resources, defining objectives, developing simulation materials, preparing facilities, displays and materials, and identifying, selecting and training staff.

The third step is the actual *conduct of the exercise* where controllers, simulators, and evaluators may be employed.

The fourth step, *Critique and Evaluation*, is a debriefing of all participants immediately after the exercise.

Step five, *Follow-up*, involves ensuring that issues identified in the evaluation are addressed and ready for re-examination in the next appropriate exercise. Steps four and five will be presented in greater detail.

EXERCISE EVALUATION

Exercise evaluation and follow-up go hand in hand, since for any suggested changes to be of any benefit they must be acted upon. This, after all, is the purpose of evaluation and follow-up.

The general items the evaluation seeks to assess are:
- the general appropriateness of the plan;
- whether the emergency management system employed is adequate;
- the training of staff, volunteers and key decision-makers;
- the adequacy of equipment and resources;, and, whether the exercise has achieved its objective(s).

In step two of the five-step exercise development process, specific objectives for the particular exercise were developed. These really serve their purpose at the end of the exercise when the exercise's efficacy is reviewed: did it achieve what was intended? This is a procedural evaluation which really looks at the exercise process itself. This is important to keep the cost and expenditure of time on track.

The actual evaluation of the decisions, communications, resource allocation and other strategic decisions are the other half of the evaluation. This is where questions are addressed, such as, are additional resources necessary? Are parts of the plan in need of revision? Is additional training required? Are staffing levels adequate? Is the communication system vulnerable to overload? Can first response units communicate with one another?[6]

After an exercise the question arises of when to report on the evaluation. The literature seems to identify two approaches and often recommends they be used together. The first is the immediate critique which is done as soon as possible after the exercise ends. This has the benefit of the issues and problems being fresh in everyone's mind and allows a general discussion by all participants. It is important that the tone of the discussion remain positive by highlighting successes and viewing problems as weaknesses (or opportunities) for future improvement. Further, personal criticisms must not be tolerated as they only serve to inject negative and hostile reactions. Part of this immediate critique should also include a one-on-one by the evaluator and persons in essential positions to candidly, yet positively, review both people's perceptions of how that function was played. These should be kept brief and touch on the major issues only. The immediate critique is largely for self-learning where players generally report their own faults or problems and is mostly just facilitated by the evaluator.

The second approach is the evaluation report. This is written days or weeks after the exercise and is based upon the evaluator's notes from his or her observations during the exercise. This is the place for the evaluator to deal with larger more general issues and problems and not so much the smaller personal-level issues addressed in the immediate critique, although these should still be included for reference, perhaps as an appendix to the report. It is the opportunity for the evaluator to make written recommendations after thoughtful consideration of how best to remedy any shortcomings. It is a formal report which is to be circulated to all participants in the exercise and finally to be put before the Emergency Program Planning Committee for action.

Although follow-up is a logical consequence after the critical evaluation of an exercise, the evaluation process will be for naught if the recommendations for action are not completed. Assigning responsibility for such follow-up must be made. Since the formal report is submitted to the Emergency Program Planning Committee for action, it is logical for this body to determine which recommendation will be acted upon and ensuring the action items are addressed. The Emergency Program Coordinator, being the functionary of this committee as well as being the resident emergency planning resource, should undertake the task of working with those responsible for effecting the required changes if they do not fall within the scope of the Emergency Program Coordinator.

Exercise planning is a very involved process. What has been outlined here are the basics necessary to understanding and planning for emergency plan exercises. Some jurisdictions will offer specific courses on the conduct of certain kinds of exercises discussed here. The reader wishing to pursue more detailed reading on the conduct of exercises should consult **Disaster Recovery Testing: Exercising Your Contingency Plan** (Philip Jan Rothstein, editor), **Emergency Exercise Handbook: Evaluate and Integrate Your Company's Plan** (Tracy Knippenburg Gillis) or **Exercise Planning and Evaluation** (Patrick Lavalla).

SENIOR LEVEL SUPPORT AND PARTICIPATION

Finally, a brief note about the role of senior level managers in exercises and their evaluations. Emergency planning must be recognized as the priority issue that it is and must have senior managers fully participating in both exercises and evaluations for them to be both realistic and to have credibility for other managers and staff to fully participate. This, however, puts a challenge on the shoulders of the exercise planners to make exercises relevant and concise, to insure they are executed without undue delays and that only the necessary staff are involved for the type of exercise chosen.

Given these objectives, senior managers should be able to take time away from their busy schedules for complete participation. This will provide the full degree of realism for the exercise as well as doing immense benefit for the emergency program in conveying to other staff that this is an important undertaking and has complete support right to the top of the management structure. Obviously, without such support exercises will achieve very little other than providing the opportunity for practice in planning an exercise, rather than the conduct of a mock emergency.

CONTINUING RESPONSIBILITY

Once the pieces have come together, that is planning, education, training and exercising, the local government should be able to feel confident that it has done every reasonable thing in preparation. This does not mean, however, that emergency planning and preparedness can be forgotten about.

EMERGENCY PROGRAM PLANNING COMMITTEE

The Emergency Program Planning Committee should be a standing committee that meets regularly, (at least twice annually if all of the above have been completed), to provide an oversight function over emergency preparedness within the local government's jurisdiction.

It has already been made clear that this committee has a responsibility to meet annually to review the emergency program for continued relevance, focus and practicality. However, this committee does not remain in a suspended state between annual reviews: a clear and continuing responsibility should be entrenched in the enabling bylaw or ordinance stating this obligation. Meetings should be called as needed to address any significant changes in the nature of the threats against the community, or significant changes in important personnel, operating procedures or emergency procedures within the local government. Such matters should be addressed for their strategic impact on the existing program of plan relevance, public information, training requirements and exercise scheduling.

The constitution of committee membership will continue to provide that important cross-section of emergency response agencies within the community so that any significant change in the capability of any member agency would be brought forward for assessment.

EMERGENCY PROGRAM COORDINATOR

The Emergency Program Coordinator remains as the eyes and ears of the Emergency Program Planning Committee, especially when all is said and done and the committee meets on a reduced basis. Remaining in close contact on an ongoing basis with each Emergency Program Planning Committee agency and keeping an eye out for changes in the status or availability of those community resources identified in some plans are primary tasks, in addition to either directly facilitating or prompting sub-committees in exercise planning, and consulting on training matters.

While this sounds onerous, it is almost of a housekeeping nature if thorough and sufficient work by the Emergency Program Planning Committee and its sub-committees has gone into planning training requirements and setting the exercise schedule. Only in large local governments is the Emergency Program Coordinator typically a dedicated, full-time resource. In most local governments, the Emergency Program Coordinator will have other, often significant, corporate responsibilities. Time must be made for emergency program matters and the astute Emergency Program Coordinator will keep such duties salient in ones mind during the execution of these other duties. Meeting with various groups, travel around the community and intelligence gleaned from fellow managers within the local government all contribute to the ability to keep abreast of significant changes that will impact the Comprehensive Emergency Management Plan.

Finally, close liaison with the Emergency Program Planning Committee chairperson will determine if and when the committee needs to meet to discuss certain matters. Generally, information is compiled slowly, and to amass enough information to necessitate a meeting of the committee may see it meet twice annually to discuss changes which, really, amount to its annual review.

THE PLAN IN FINAL FORM

The final product, the Comprehensive Emergency Management Plan, is a useful tool, but, like most tools, is only useful to those familiar with it. This familiarity cannot be instilled if it sits on a shelf forgotten about or worse, providing a local government with a false sense of security. Every aspect of this document, the process, and the subsequent training and exercising, should be part of regular activities within the local government. Calling aspects of the plan into use for a multitude of uses, such as major sporting events, should not be discouraged. It provides certain things, such as a command and control system, which are useful in non-emergency situations. This will help keep it current, relevant and known to all who use it.

FINAL WORD: DYNAMIC EMERGENCIES REQUIRE DYNAMIC PLANS

Finally, local governments should keep in mind that dynamic emergencies require dynamic plans. While particular components of the overall Comprehensive

Emergency Management Plan are the best pre-emergency guess at what will be required and how the emergency will be addressed, one must be flexible to allow the best response to emerge. This requires not slavishly adhering to what was an educated guess as to how things would unfold. The plan gets you to the emergency and provides that initial direction.

If thorough planning, training and exercise result in the plan being used as it was written then this entire process has achieved its goal. However, if the plan has not been sufficiently or thoroughly exercised, or the evolution of the emergency dictates a departure from that plan, this should be allowed and the course of action noted for a subsequent rewrite of the plan, since an actual emergency deployment is the best exercise of them all and affords the greatest learning opportunity.

CONCLUSION

This work has attempted to span a very large topic. Books have been written on each aspect of *Comprehensive Emergency Management* and the reader should not be under the illusion that this work is exhaustive or authoritative. It is, however, an attempt to distill from that body of literature and debate, a simple and straightforward approach to local government emergency planning that touches on each of the important areas of consideration which ultimately leads to a reliable Comprehensive Emergency Management Plan.

Key Points

- Four phases of *Comprehensive Emergency Management*: mitigation, preparedness, response and recovery
- Plan development is 20%, education and training 30%, and exercising 50%
- Never rely on a plan until it has been exercised
- The public should be educated on the nature of hazards faced by the community. Local government staff should be models of personal and family preparedness
- Participants in emergency management, either planning or operations, need proper training
- Exercising the plan is essential as it promotes preparedness, tests plans and procedures, trains personnel and instils the plan in the minds of the key managers
- Five types of exercises: orientation, drill, tabletop, functional and full-scale
- Thorough evaluation of exercises is important to extract the maximum benefit
- The Emergency Program Coordinator maintains a continuous presence by observing changes in the organization and community that have a bearing on the emergency plan
- The Emergency Program Planning Committee also has an ongoing presence in monitoring and guiding the direction of the overall emergency program

[1] "The Need For Exercises and Types of Exercises" unpublished handout by Ross McIntyre, Justice Institute of B.C. January 1995.

[2] *ibid.*

[3] "Exercising Business Continuation Plans Without Training and Exercise, Your Plan is Wasted" by Rick Lawson in Municipal Insurance Association Newsletter *Exchange*. May 2000.

[4] Taken from Exercise Process course manual. Justice Institute of B.C. February 1997.

[5] *ibid.*

[6] *ibid.*

APPENDIX A:

SAMPLE PLANNING OUTLINE

I. Mitigation - This is one of the most important elements of Comprehensive Emergency Management, as it identifies the potential emergencies that may befall a community. At this stage, be thorough and deliberate in all information gathering and analysis. Overlooking a hazard as a potential emergency may be magnified in the long term as planning effort and resources are devoted to identified threats. The overlooked ones may lurk like sharks in the water only to surprise your community when it is vulnerable.

   A. Objectives - There are four objectives of mitigation that are all-inclusive and should not need to be supplemented.

      1. Eliminate Hazards - Some hazards can be eliminated. While it is possible to eliminate some natural hazards by, for example, constructing flood control systems or engineering slope stability solutions, this section largely refers to the human-generated hazards such as movement of hazardous materials or securing vulnerable critical infrastructure against penetration.

      2. Reduce Risks - Where hazards cannot be eliminated, the risk of an occurrence can be reduced. This can have two aspects: immediate action and long-term planning. Immediate action can include assessing a hazardous operation to rationalize or streamline it thereby reducing the risk exposure; For example, reducing the number of vehicle trips of hazardous materials by consolidating trips for maximum efficiency/minimum risk. Over the long-term, hazard mitigation should be included as a fundamental aspect of community planning.

3. **Reduce Consequences** - There are two aspects: impact and response. Impact involves coming to terms with the inevitable by employing certain engineering design elements, such as seismic retrofitting, blast proofing or fire resistance. Response involves enhancing the emergency services capability to an appropriate level or standard. This includes hazard-specific preparedness plans, training, exercising, specific equipment and wisely locating such resources for prompt deployment.

4. **Spread Risks** - Legally, local governments may have a difficult time trying to achieve clear contractual transfer of liability. Indeed, in some jurisdictions this is forbidden by law (see *Risk Management*). However, risk and liability can be attenuated to some degree by downloading information and expectations to those likely to be affected by a particular hazard. This involves public education, promoting personal preparedness, advertising the role/use of local emergency plans, raising awareness of specific hazards, demanding of covenants and other encumbrances such as written acknowledgement of persons undertaking activities or building in hazard-prone areas.

B. **Risk Assessment** - There are two elements to Risk Assessment: identifying the hazard and then estimating how an impact will affect the community.

1. **Hazard Identification** - This includes anything that will have an adverse effect on the community by threatening lives, infrastructure, facilities, critical service delivery, or potential to generate casualties or evacuees. Hazards may be either internal or external to the community. An all-hazards approach is recommended.

a. **Internal Hazards** - These are hazards that may occur within the community as would be the case in the majority of local government emergencies. These would include items coming under three broad headings: natural hazards, human-caused hazards and social hazards.

b. **External Hazards** - These are potential emergencies occurring elsewhere than within the community but which have a significant impact on that community nevertheless. Such scenarios may see a large influx of evacuees or casualties, or the secondment of key staff and the use of mutual aid agreements. These situations may be rare but have the possibility of overwhelming local services and systems, specifically certain critical services and thereby restricting access of local residents.

c. **Hazard Inventory** - This has two aspects: enumerating the hazards that face a community and ranking the probability of occurrence. Comprehensive lists of hazards are widely available for use as a checklist in any community. The determination of probability may be a combination of local traditional knowledge and scientific investigation.

2. **Vulnerability Analysis** - The assessment of how the impact of a particular hazard will affect your community. This must be thought of from two perspectives: the effect on citizens and the effect on the response systems.

a. **Impact Assessment** - This is the impact on a number of critical sectors.

   i. **Types of Impacts**

      Social - Impacts such as number of deaths and injuries, loss of housing and disruption of education.

      Environmental - This includes effects on air and water quality, vegetation and wildlife.

      Economic - This would include such things as structural and non-structural damage, loss of infrastructure and transportation systems, loss of crops and other work in progress, and loss of jobs.

      Political - Minimize the opportunity for the any perception of blame and allow for the elected representatives to be seen in their leadership role. Also, allow for a "chain of command" if certain key people are away or incapacitated.

   ii. **Systems Impacted** - Any impact will affect the "systems" upon which a community operates and which may ultimately be affected and must be planned for.

- **Regulatory** - Regulatory systems may be changed temporarily during an emergency and permanently afterwards. This includes freedom of movement, public health and industry regulation. This may also result from the involvement of senior levels of government.

- **Human** - The human environment will most certainly be altered during an emergency as individual lives will be conducted under abnormal circumstances and will be affected in the long-term as a result of the psychological trauma from the emergency.

- **Building** - The built environment usually suffers under most hazard scenarios. Flood-proofing, seismic retrofitting and slope stability are areas of common focus.

- **Business** - Commercially, individual enterprises may be affected, some of which may never re-open. Certain commercial services may be in high demand and short supply during and after an emergency. The business side of local government service delivery requires attention under this assessment (see *Service Continuation Plan*).

b. **Ethnic and Cultural Consideration** - Multicultural communities must consider delivery of critical information in languages other than English. English-as-a-second-language citizens may have difficulty understanding directions, relating critical information or availing themselves of support services. Larger communities deliver services in a dozen or more languages. Local government staff members of certain ethnic groups are invaluable assets in this regard.

C. Risk Management - Risk management is the balance of continuing to do business "as is" across the spectrum of local government services versus taking diversionary measures to mitigate hazard impact.

1. Types of Losses - Four categories of losses:

a. Personnel - This is the loss of key people within a service delivery system that has an adverse impact on the ability to continue that service. Identify alternate people and have them cross-trained in key positions.

b. Property - This is the loss of equipment, supplies or facilities of an organization due to theft or damage from natural or negligent acts.

c. Expenses - The expense incurred due to an emergency that are not reimbursed through senior levels of government are losses under Risk Management.

d. Liability - These are personnel, property or expense losses of others due to alleged negligent acts by the local government. Local governments should make it expressly clear that employees or agents are no longer indemnified by the corporation if they are found to be acting in a negligent manner.

2. Five Steps - There is distinct five-step process to Risk Management:

a. Identify Exposures - This largely overlaps with hazard identification although an additional consideration here is liability exposure through statutory obligations.

b. Examine Risk Management Techniques - Two approaches: risk and risk financing.

i. Risk Control - This uses control measures to minimize potential losses. Each of the identified exposures should be screened against the five risk control techniques.

- **Exposure Avoidance** - The objective here is to reduce the probability of risk to zero; therefore, the discretionary activities must be critically reviewed to determine if certain activities of varying risk are worth continuing to undertake or offer.

- **Loss Prevention** - If reduction to zero is not feasible, then reduce the number of times an activity is undertaken to minimize the risk and any subsequent loss.

- **Loss Reduction** - Even at a reduced frequency, local government activities will be impacted by risky activities. Loss reduction aims to limit the severity of an impact. This involves off-site storage of back-up records, mutual aid agreements, etc.

- **Segregation of Expenditures** - This is the "don't-keep-all-your-eggs-in-one-basket" approach. Critical supplies, services and personnel should be separated to a number of facilities where possible to eliminate one major emergency at one facility from becoming catastrophic.

- **Contractual Transfer** - This transfers the risk exposure to a contractor. While not available to local governments for their core functions, it is a useful tool in routine contracts that the supplier take on this exposure, e.g. gas and chemical delivery, toxic waste disposal, etc.

ii. **Risk Financing** - This approach accepts that certain losses are inevitable and retains some form of insurance to cover such. This can be done through commercial insurance or self-insurance on part of the local government.

c. **Select Best Technique(s)** - Different service functions will have different risk management options that work best for each. In arriving at that decision, four criteria are generally used as a screening tool: technical feasibility; financial constraints; legal requirements; and, humanitarian considerations.

d. **Implement Selected Technique(s)** - Risk management techniques must be implemented to be useful.

There are two dimensions to implementation: technical - where input from a wide range of experts is sought; and, managerial - where the implementation strategies are derived that support successful transition to the new paradigm. This area requires a great amount of time and is really a long-term consideration. The technical side is relatively easy to sort out and to arrive at a proper course of action. For this new approach to be sustainable and successful, senior management must support it fully and commit immediately to the necessary elements of cultural change to support those change agents within the organization.

e. Monitor and Revise Approach - The need for a change of risk management technique over time may occur, or the implementation may not be developing as envisioned. Likewise, the nature of service delivery changes and new tasks are undertaken. Regular review of the risk management process will ensure that it is serving its purpose by continuing to be relevant and accurate. The risk management process should set out a program of review with a mandate, supported by senior management, to facilitate change in this program as needed.

D. Risk Communication - The knowledge of risk should not be confined to just a few. Broad communication of risk, risks posed to the community, what steps the local government has taken and what steps members of the public can take to minimize personal exposure to risk, should be undertaken.

1. Education - As much information as possible on hazards, threats, risk, preparedness, response and recovery should be passed on to local government staff and the general public. Such education established a broad base of support for the emergency program and develops an element of self-reliance.

a. Staff - Apprise staff of likely scenarios, mitigation and planning efforts, and the unique role they play as individual emergency survivors and then local government service providers. This undertaking should anticipate how best to accomplish this.

b. Public - The important element in public education is post-emergency public health threats, the availability of health care facilities and techniques for avoiding becoming a victim (e.g., personal and family preparedness lists). This can be identified as part of an on-going annual emergency program public education campaign.

2. Prevention - Prevention should be everyone's business. It should be acknowledged in mitigation efforts and specifically in a coordinated public education campaign. The EPC (, however, should play an active role in prevention/mitigation by being involved in numerous aspects of community development. He/she has a unique perspective to offer in identifying potential catastrophic problems of an emergency management nature lost on other professionals focussing closely on their spheres of expertise. Authority should be established for such a role under this section.

II. Preparedness Plan - This is the most multiple-faceted aspect of Comprehensive Emergency Management. The preparedness plan is a collection of a number of sub-plans each with a specific objective. These plans provide the general emergency management framework and plans for addressing specific hazards.

A. Emergency Management Plan - This is the hub of the preparedness plan. It provides the flexile management system that enables decision makers to react to any emergency situation even in the absence of any hazard-specific preparedness plan.

1. Table of Contents - A table of contents is useful to show the organization of the emergency plan and allows for the quick location of important items under stressful situations when even the most obvious heading is overlooked in haste.

2. Distribution List - This serves two purposes: It allows the EPC to track who has been issued a copy of the plan which easily facilitates the distribution of updates, and it allows users of the plan to know who should be familiar with its contents. To assist in ensuring that users have the current version of the plan, have the date of the current version on the cover and as a footer on every page. This will be useful in updating the entire plan or an individual page.

3. Mayor's Endorsement - This statement solidifies support for the plan, the program and its objectives. The top office in the organization, whether called by a different name or not, must put his/her support behind this effort for it to be efficacious.

4. Authority - It is important to establish the basis for undertaking this authority. In some jurisdictions it is a statutory obligation while in others it is simply prudent preparation. Specifically reference any Act of senior government and any bylaw, ordinance or policy of the local government establishing the program. If no such local enactment, one should be put in place to properly establish the authority for the necessary expenditures and secondments.

5. Scope - This briefly outlines what the plan is intended to address. In keeping with the principle of this book, be sure to make clear that this plan is to be used as often as possible and should not be reserved for the very rare big emergency. Common use will yield a familiarity that will be critical in larger emergencies.

6. Authorization - Although it is intended to be used frequently, the plan cannot be deployed carelessly. A carefully thought out activation procedure must be articulated to ensure its use is appropriately sanctioned and supported. This does not always have to be initiated by political figures unless required by local law. The senior administrator or a delegate should be capable of authorizing such.

7. Line of Succession - Regardless of who authorizes deployment (use) of the Emergency Management Plan, the EPC will be a central figure. A deployment cannot be hampered by the absence or unavailability of the EPC so a number of alternates should be identified. It is critical that those alternates be fully capable of fulfilling all duties of the EPC.

8. Activation - This section sets out for the response agencies an idea of how the plan is activated. It is recommended that the emergency service, or perhaps a centralized dispatch, contact the EPC, or alternate as appropriate, to advise of a particular situation and the need for some form of support or coordination (hence the use of the plan). The appropriateness of use of the plan can quickly be discussed, and a determination made if it is necessary. If so, the EPC facilitates the securing of authorization to deploy the plan and the setup/activation of the EOC. Support then flows to the incident as needed. One brief call to the EPC is all the response agencies should need to make. Beyond this, the EPC fulfils his/her duties.

9. **Role of the Emergency Operations Center** - It is very important for everyone's benefit to state definitively the role of the EOC. The role of the EOC is to support the responders in the field. This may be one incident or multiple incidents. The support and coordination of resources for maximum benefit are best coordinated from this distance from the scene of the incident(s).

10. **Hazard Analysis** - This references work undertaken in the mitigation section and links the greatest hazards to hazard-specific preparedness plans. Its purpose is to let the reader know that a review of potential hazards has been undertaken.

11. **Public Information** - Public information in time of emergency is critical and should be taken seriously by the local government. Manifesting it as a priority here in the plan simply reinforces its priority and prominent position to users of the plan. The Emergency Public Information Plan is detailed later.

12. **Annual Review** - As with Public Information, inclusion of this heading is simply a way of committing the plan to an annual review as a matter of priority. A great deal can be learned in the course of a year through actual use of the plan, exercises, mitigation and training. Also, the nature of some hazards may change necessitating changes to the plan. Annual review must occur to avoid the plan rapidly becoming out of date.

13. **Emergency Operations Center** - The EOC is the control point for any emergencies that occur within the local government jurisdiction. As such, it is important that its layout and operation be known and understood by all, in particular those primary and alternate staff who will be required to attend it.

    a. **Purpose** - The purpose is to act as the command center for any emergency within the jurisdiction. Under ICS, incident commanders retain control over all activity at the scene. The EOC plays a higher level of command and control by supporting that incident commander and coordinating resources and large-scale strategic planning in multiple-incident scenarios.

    b. **Location** - State the location of the primary and any alternate EOCs. EOCs may be permanently set up rooms waiting for activation or, as in most small communities, it is the rapid conversion of an existing conference room. The EPC must ensure that all required supplies and resources are easily and quickly accessible for such a set up.

c. Staffing - List those who need to be in the EOC. List them by position title rather than name to avoid problems with staff turnover. Identify secondary and tertiary alternates. EOC members should be persons who can contribute in a constructive manner to the response phase of an emergency. The text suggests a list of typical members although membership will vary by jurisdiction and be affected by nuances of the emergency management system employed.

d. Prolonged Operations - EOC operations can range from one person functioning during business hours only to a large operation functioning twenty-four hours per day. Once operations go beyond operating eight to twelve hours per day over several consecutive days, relief staff need to be employed. These will normally be the secondary or tertiary alternates identified above.

e. Equipment - List the equipment the EOC needs to operate (suggested in text). The basics are not extensive but are fundamental to smooth sustained operation. This equipment for a fully deployed EOC operating on a continuous basis for a prolonged period should be available either in a dedicated room or stored away within an existing and suitable conference room.

f. Liability Issues - Like Public Information and Annual Review, this point is included as a reminder to plan users and EOC members of liability issues that can arise from emergency response. Individuals and emergency service representatives in the EOC must use logbooks to detail actions taken and at what time. The EOC Recording Clerk maintains a log of all major occurrences and actions taken, provides log sheets to EOC members and collect these afterwards. Part of the EPC's duties is to ensure that log sheets are routinely being filled out.

14. State of Local Emergency - This section presents the highest state that a local government can declare in an emergency response. How this is done and what extraordinary powers it entails will vary by jurisdiction, however, the fact that it can be done (to whatever the extent) is worth noting.

a. **Declaration of State of Local Emergency** - The source of the authority to declare such should be noted and the procedure for doing so detailed (best if verbatim from the enabling Act). It should comment on for how long it is valid and how citizens will be notified of such.

b. **Powers of Council during a State of Local Emergency** - Where practical an if not too extensive, the powers assumed by the local government should be included. This saves the EPC searching through an Act looking to verify a clause and clearly identifies them for the elected officials in order to plan what extraordinary measures can best be employed to address a certain situation.

c. **Cancellation of a State of Local Emergency** - Like Declaration, the procedure for cancelling a state of local emergency should be noted and how citizens will be informed. A vital role of the EPC at this time is how to inform all responders that the response is back under "normal" rules.

15. **Appendices** - The Preparedness Plan is intended to be all-inclusive; therefore, certain appendices must be included to achieve this objective while others are memory aids or time savers.

a. **Responsibilities During and After an Emergency** - This is a useful aid to members of the EOC that serves two purposes: it lists the responsibilities of each member and serves as a checklist of immediate actions upon deployment of the EOC. It should detail all actions the EOC members should undertake before, during and after an emergency.

b. **Emergency Telephone Call Out List** - An accurate and up-to-date telephone contact list of all members of the EOC and their alternate should be maintained by the EPC as an appendix to the Emergency Management Plan. Being a callout list, this is the list the EPC will use to contact and muster the EOC members. Depending on the extent of the list, a "fan-out" procedure may be used where the EPC contacts a fixed number of people who each in turn contact another number of people. Keep it up-to-date and accurate with at least two alternates for each position.

c. **Emergency Public Information Plan** - Include this plan in its entirety. Details follow later.

d. **Emergency Social Services Plan** - same as above

e. **Evacuation Plan** - same as above

f. **Emergency Telecommunications Plan** - same as above

g. **Hazard-Specific Preparedness Plans** - same as above

h. **Declaration of State of Local Emergency** - This is a template that conforms to the requirements of the enabling statute. It speeds the declaration process if it is a "fill-in-the-blanks" design. When done in advance it should conform fully to the requirements.

i. **Evacuation Order** - Like the declaration, done in advance it saves time when needed and will be clearly worded.

j. **Notice of Evacuation Order** - As above, a prepared notice saves time, carries appropriate wording and serves a legal purpose of establishing that proper and sufficient notice was given.

k. **Mutual Aid Agreement(s)** - Depending on the situation with regard to local resources, mutual aid agreements may be needed to provide specific items or to supplement local resources. For ease of reference, all mutual aid agreements should be included in this appendix.

l. **Community Resource Inventory** - This list is difficult to maintain with a high degree of accuracy and comprehensiveness, but is worth the effort. During an emergency, anything can be requested so a list of resources available in the community with contact telephone numbers may be worthwhile. This should include dump trucks, excavators, sand, pumps, etc. Such a list will grow over time and periodic checks of items and telephone numbers will maintain a reasonable degree of accuracy.

B. **Common Priority Plans** - The following four plans are important tools that support the general Emergency Management Plan. Each of these four is either a priority committed to in the Emergency Management Plan or is of such broad application that they may be employed in any of the emergencies that may befall a community.

1. **Emergency Public Information Plan** - Keeping citizens informed is an absolute necessity. Accordingly, this should be the second planning task. Ensure that this plan is efficient and use it in every emergency.

   a. **Purpose** - The purpose of this plan is to inform citizens of the jurisdiction about the extent of, and response to, any emergency affecting the community.

   b. **Annual Review** - As with all plans, this plan should be committed to an annual review to ensure procedures remain appropriate and media contact telephone numbers are accurate.

   c. **Scope** - This plan will find application in every emergency within the jurisdiction. Where important information does not need to be passed along to the public, the media will be inquiring to carry the story in/on their next edition as a news item.

   d. **Concept of Operation** - This is the statement of how the plan will fulfil its purpose. In this case the release of information and the focal point for media/citizen enquiries will be the Emergency Public Information Center (EPIC).

   e. **Objectives** - These reflect the priorities of the local government with respect to emergency public information. For example, these may include a timely deployment of the EPIC, to establish immediate contact with identified media outlets, to anticipate and prepare for the information needs of citizens, to provide timely updates to citizens about response actions, to immediately provide a telephone number for information, to foster an on-going working relationship with the media, etc.

   f. **Activation** - Outline who contacts whom to deploy this plan. This decision does not need to be reserved for the Chief Administrative Officer. The EPC should contact the Public Information Officer (PIO) once the former has been notified of an emergency. These two should then decide the scale of deployment of the plan.

   g. **Callout Procedure** - The EPC will contact the PIO who can in turn contact his staff and volunteers as needed. As with any telephone callout list, it must be maintained accurately and tested by calling each number at least twice yearly.

h. Public Information Officer - This designated official will be a public information professional if the local government has one on staff. Otherwise, it can be the local government Clerk or Secretary. This individual should receive training in media relations.

    i. Duties - Specify the duties and responsibilities for this position. These may include activating the plan, calling out staff, deploying the EPIC, control and coordination of information releases, establishing a call center as needed, liaison with the media, etc.

    ii. Immediate Action Checklist - Those duties required to be executed immediately by the PIO should be in the form of an immediate action checklist. This may even be in the form of a plasticized wallet card for quick reference.

i. Emergency Public Information Center - This is the physical location that the media will attend for briefings, through which news releases will be made, and where the public will call for information. It is staffed by the PIO and his/her staff.

    i. Public Information Clerk - This person is the administrative hub of the EPIC. He/she assists in the set up of the facility, coordinates the set up of media briefings, supervises/operates information telephone lines, prepares news releases, and logs the major activities of the EPIC.

    ii. Location and Alternate - The location of the EPIC should be specified along with an alternate location. The site selected should allow for suitable office space for the administration of the EPIC; contain a suitably sized conference room where public officials can speak to the media; contain a waiting area for media representatives; be physically secure from unauthorized entry into the

EOC or other sensitive areas; and, allow for a number of telephone operators should a call center need to be established.

iii. **Equipment** - Detail the supplies that will be needed so the clerk will know what specifically needs to be provided. Consult the PIO and his staff on the supplies and equipment they will require to perform their tasks.

iv. **Layout** - This will vary with each location and the extent to which the site can fulfil the desired layout mentioned under Location. Include a layout of the primary and alternate locations right in the plan itself.

v. **Prolonged Operations** - The use of the EPIC may vary from a few hours each day to twenty-four hours per day when a call center is employed. Accordingly, relief staff must be trained in order to sustain the operation. The PIO and the clerk have specialized functions whereas telephone operators can be trained quickly and provided with a pre-approved statement for release.

vi. **Media Accreditation** - The plan must identify how duly accredited media representatives will be identified. Part of the equipment/supplies for the EPIC should include the ability to produce readily identifiable but not easily reproducible identification badges. Before credentials are issued, the validity of the individual representing a media interest should be verified. This can be achieved by liaison with local media and major networks to identify a list of people who may be assigned. Producing identification for the individual is all that is then required when they arrive at the EPIC. Out-of-town media may require a telephone call to verify their status if not "pre-approved." This, of course, may prove difficult during a major emergency.

j. Call Center - The extent of the call center may vary depending on the size of the local government jurisdiction and the severity of the emergency.

   i. Location - Although usually desirable to have this co-located with the EPIC, this is not also practical in some circumstances. The primary consideration is that the call center has sufficient space for the number of operators required. Industrial psychologists are able to identify ideal working conditions. In this case, however, austerity will be a factor. Each operator will require sufficient personal space and a comfortable chair and desk or table to work at as a minimum. It would be preferred if there were no outside visibility to distract them (i.e., viewing the emergency), which would also help to protect them from debris in such cases as tornadoes, etc.

   ii. Volunteers - The human side of a call center is scalable as volunteers usually are plentiful and can be trained easily. Supervision is the key to ensure all operators pass along the current information accurately.

   iii. Technical Issues - The technical side of a call center is the greatest concern. The PIO should identify a call centre location (and alternate) and work closely with the local telephone company to put in place a multiple-line telephone system that can be activated easily to supplement the existing telephone system. This usually involves pre-wiring the call center locations with multiple phone jacks that can be activated at the telephone switch for that building. Stored away in that room should be a corresponding number of telephones. The number of units should be sufficient to handle a moderate sized emergency. This will allow for partial activation in a small emergency, sufficient coverage for moderate sized emergencies, but could be overwhelmed in a large emergency. To put in place a sufficient number of units for a major emergency may not be justifiable given their rare occurrence.

k. Appendices

i. Media Outlets and Contacts - In order for the PIO to be proactive in dealing with the media, an accurate and up-to-date contact list of all relevant media outlets should be kept. Check this regularly for reliability as both telephone numbers and individuals change over time. This may also double as a pre-authorization list of media contacts who may be assigned.

ii. EPIC Staff Contact Numbers - This relates to the telephone callout procedure. The professional or seconded staff generally will be a few people. The supervisor of the call center can be made responsible for calling/recruiting volunteers as needed.

iii. News Release Template - A reproducible blank news release template is useful. This allows hasty news releases to be done by hand, particularly when the power is interrupted, although every effort should be made to present them professionally. Important information to contain is the date and time of release, and who to contact for further information.

2. Emergency Social Services Plan - The ESS Plan is the next critical plan as the local government must be prepared to address the human needs at all times.

a. Purpose - The purpose of this plan is to provide for registration of displaced persons; their shelter, food and clothing if needed; the inquiries of loved ones as to the status of a displaced person; and, to support the EOC and the incident site, when safe to do so, with the provision of food and other support services.

b. Annual Review - This plan needs an annual review to ensure the various suppliers and service/social clubs are still active and interested in continuing their support role.

c. **Scope** - A properly written ESS plan should be expandable to meet the particular need. This may range from the provision of meals in support of prolonged EOC operations to running evacuation centers housing significant populations for extended periods.

d. **Concept of Operation** - How will this plan achieve its stated purpose? It will do so through the intelligent identification of facilities sited such that they will serve the greatest population yet be as emergency resistant as possible; through the pre-selection of suppliers of critical resources; through the strategic stockpiling of certain resources; and, the recruitment and training of volunteers.

e. **Objectives** - Like any objective, these should be simple, achievable and measurable. In the case of Emergency Social Services, these should include the rapid opening of reception centers in or near affected areas, and the prompt establishment of registration and inquiry services.

f. **Activation** - While this plan should be activated as early as possible in anticipation of the need of its services, it must be activated upon proper authority as that deployment has a cost and will possibly disrupt the use of specific facilities. Therefore, once the Emergency Program Coordinator is apprised of an emergency and then seeks the necessary approval to activate the Emergency Management Plan, he/she should also seek approval to deploy the ESS Plan if, in the EPC's opinion, it is or would likely be required.

g. **Callout Procedure** - For either the activation of the plan or the stand-by of the ESS staff, the Emergency Program Coordinator will contact the ESS Director. The ESS Director can then place key managers on his/her staff on standby or issue orders for the activation of various parts of that plan. Each manager will in turn contact those staff members or volunteers as needed. A contact sheet of names and alternates along with their telephone numbers should be retained by the director and the managers.

h. Emergency Lodging - This is one of the three important areas of ESS. A manager should be assigned to each of these three tasks to coordinate its provision. Lodging and feeding can be a combination of on-site provision or commercially provided. Clothing involves private donation and assistance through established charities. Each area is a very detailed job unto itself; however, the one important element of each is public health. Public health officials should be an integral part of any such deployment to ensure anything supplied to displaced person is of a usable/consumable quality.

i. Emergency Feeding - see above

j. Emergency Clothing - see above

k. Registration and Inquiry - This is the single most important service provided in the ESS Plan. Even if displaced persons have the means to look after themselves once evacuated from their residence (i.e., staying with a family member or friend), the registration of this fact and the ability to inform inquiring loved ones is crucial. Therefore, this plan must have a highly organized supervisor and staff to undertake this task. Computers are of great assistance. Prepare for all conditions by having hardcopy forms, battery-powered laptop computers and desktop computers.

l. Individual and Family Services - Citizens may require assistance with the many aspects of the emergency that has occurred. This may include how to locate missing loved ones to counselling on coming to terms with what has occurred and how they may have been personally affected. Such services should be identified and provided for in the plan.

i. Support Agencies and Personnel - The agencies within the community that can provide these types of services should be listed. They should be contacted in the planning process to determine their ability to meet this need. Contact information must be included.

m. Reception Center Administration - Reception centers can be extremely hectic places when in full operation. Accordingly, efficient and effective management is required to allow the various sub-functions noted above to occur smoothly yet in a coordinated manner.

n. Communications - Communications between the reception center(s) and the Emergency Operations Center is important. This can best be achieved by highest level of communications available at the time. The nature of the communications is the passing of lists of names of registered persons or lists of resources required. E-mail is useful for this although facsimile also works. In the absence of these, voice over the telephone may have to suffice. Usually reserved as a last resort, Amateur Radio is surprisingly useful with its packet radio capability. Ultimately battery-powered radio voice or packet is a final option before considering a runner.

o. Additional Supplies - This section of the plan simply flags the fact that additional or supplementary supplies will be needed to support the prolonged operation of reception centers. Bulk suppliers should be identified for resources expected to be consumed in the running of reception centers.

p. Facilities - Facilities are the core of the ESS Plan. Great care should be exercised in the selection of these to ensure they will fulfil the needs of the service providers and potential users, that they are relatively free from interference of certain emergencies (i.e., floods, wildfire), and that their prolonged use will not inhibit other equally important uses (i.e., schools).

    i. Primary - Primary facilities should be located throughout a community where they would be quickly accessible in the event of an emergency in that area. These could be local "landmarks" like community halls or recreation centers. These are the facilities that are relied upon in the majority of time such will be needed.

ii. **Secondary** - These would be back-up facilities located in a number of places. First, if those more numerous and smaller primary facilities in certain areas of the community are rendered unusable in widespread emergency, centralized and larger facilities may be identified for back-up use. Also, out-of-region facilities should be identified if not covered under mutual aid or regional support agreements.

q. **Supplies** - In addition to the specific resources required under lodging, feeding and clothing, certain supplies will be needed to effectively run reception centres. A reception center kit is a good thing to assemble. Such a kit would include banners for identifying the location as such, banners for the various stations within a center, the forms and other stationary supplies manual registration of names, and possibly the computers, laptops and Amateur Radio equipment to be employed.

r. **Extended Operations** - Once deployed, reception centers will be working continuously as long as displaced citizens need service. In order to achieve this, a shift system for staff and volunteers will need to be developed. Another consideration is the batteries (radios, computers) and gasoline (generators) for any such devices employed.

s. **Closing Down** - This element is tied to the general wind-down of operations in the recovery phase. Displaced citizens will want to return to their homes as quickly as is possible after an emergency has abated, however, experience has shown, particularly in larger cities, that some individuals move into temporary shelters in order to stay as long as possible. These may be homeless persons or people with mental disorders who enjoy the special circumstances. The sad reality is that people may have to be ejected when time has come that the facilities are no longer serving their function. A process for closing the doors on a permanent basis should be articulated.

3. **Evacuation Plan** - Certain emergencies will necessitate providing for the voluntary or mandatory evacuation of citizens. Such a plan should provide for an orderly evacuation and for addressing possible impediments that may occur.

   a. **Purpose** - the purpose of this plan is to remove citizens from the possibility of bodily injury as a result of an emergency occurring.

   b. **Annual Review** - In the case of the Evacuation Plan, the annual review not only serves the purpose of a yearly review of policies and procedures to ensure their continued relevance, it is the opportunity to review any changes to the physical development of the community that may have taken place. This may include news roads or subdivisions, road closures, and new hazards adjacent to evacuation routes.

   c. **Scope** - In keeping with the theme of this book, this plan should be employable in any scale of emergency that requires the evacuation of citizens. This may include just a few households in the event of flooding or entire sections of the community under more widespread emergencies.

   d. **Concept of Operation** - Concept of operation refers to how the plan will fulfil its purpose. This is relatively straightforward to articulate in that a notification procedure will be developed and promptly executed during an emergency. This execution may vary depending on the threat necessitating the evacuation. Where time permits the notification process can be properly executed. Under adverse conditions where time is of the absolute essence, a more expedient and less formal notification may occur.

   e. **Objectives** - These are usually straightforward with such a task-specific plan and usually revolve around timeliness and thoroughness. Prompt evacuation notice and ensuring that door-to-door check have been made (where safe to do so) are the most common. It is suggested that an objective be added about effective assistance to mobility-impaired citizens.

   f. **Activation** - Activation of this plan is linked to the type of evacuation required. Immediate evacuation is the result of a decision made by the Incident

Commander who has determined that immediate evacuation will save lives. He acts unilaterally based on his/her assessment of the emergency and should be fully supported by EOC once deployed. Anticipatory evacuations result from discussions between the EOC, the Incident Commander and technical experts in the specific hazard threat. The EOC can then recommend a voluntary evacuation or pursue the appropriate process to order a mandatory evacuation (usually through the equivalent of declaring a state of local emergency).

g. **Initial Response** - This section articulates how it is envisioned that the need to order or recommend an evacuation will arise. It identifies the need of the Incident Commander to take immediate and unilateral action under certain circumstances and how this gets relayed to the EOC which, at the time, is yet to be deployed. It also identifies various scenarios where the EOC will have the opportunity to contemplate the need for evacuation and the options for achieving such.

h. **Notification** - This section should clearly state how residents will be notified of the various type of evacuation. In all cases the media should be utilized via the Emergency Public Information Plan. In the case of immediate evacuations, the emergency services should broadcast from their public address systems this fact where it is safe to remain (an element of obviousness is expected in extreme emergencies). For anticipatory evacuations, some form of indicating a residence has been informed should be used. This could be as simple as colored ribbon tied to doorknobs which would be visible from the street. The notification procedure may be modified depending on the sense of urgency and the area or number of households to contacted.

i. **Security** - There will be two elements to provide for under this section. One involves a plan to post police or reliable alternatives, such as private security companies or local government staff, in order to cordon off the evacuated area and prevent unauthorized re-entry. The other involves police patrols where safe to do so to prevent looting.

j. Evacuation Routes - Designated evacuation routes must be identified. The EPC should work with local transportation planners and police to identify the most direct routes out of various areas or neighbourhoods within the local government jurisdiction. Routes should be of sufficient capacity to accommodate the volume of traffic to be generated from specific areas of the community. Routes should also be assessed from a vulnerability point of view to ensure that they will not be easily blocked by fallen overpasses, flooded low spots or pass any other potential hazards (refineries, pipelines, etc.)

k. Immediate Evacuation - As already mentioned, there may be a need for an immediate evacuation ordered by the Incident Commander. These maybe under various local enactments that bestow such power on Police or Fire Chiefs or can be "highly recommended" where no such specific authority exists. This eventuality should be recognized and acknowledged in the plan and provision made binding of the Incident Commander to inform the EOC immediately upon it being deployed and ready to provide support to the incident.

l. Anticipatory Evacuation - In the case of slower onset emergencies, such as flooding or approaching bad weather, anticipatory evacuations may be necessary.

   i. Voluntary - Depending upon the threat posed, the local government may suggest citizens evacuate for their own safety but cannot or choose not to make it a mandatory evacuation. Enticement to evacuate may include the establishment of reception centres and evacuation shelters at a safe distance form the emergency.

   ii. Mandatory - Where the power exists through some local Act, a mandatory evacuation may be ordered and enforced. This would be used where there exists and imminent risk of injury or death and must be supported by alternative accommodation for the evacuees.

Provisions for accomplishing this extraordinary act are included under the Emergency Management Plan as two separate appendices (Notice of Evacuation Order and Evacuation Order.

m. Immobile Persons - A complete plan should contain provision for addressing the needs of mobility-impaired citizens. This immobility may come about for several reasons which are generally of a medical mature. Some simply may need specialized transport, such as for individuals confined to wheelchairs or attached to medical equipment, while others may need medical support and transport via ambulance. Buses from a transit company set up for this type of transport should be listed as a resource and discussions with the local ambulance provider should be undertaken to allow for their assistance notwithstanding their role in responding to the primary emergency.

n. Appendices

i. Route Clearing Heavy Equipment - The plan should anticipate the blockage of routes under different emergency scenarios. This should include equipment to address snow, fallen trees, power lines, landslides, etc. Flooded routes are more difficult to deal with. Where possible, pumps can be used to drain limited areas where they of vital importance.

ii. Mass Transportation Resources - Any private and public transit companies, including the use of school buses when not used for school purposes, should be contacted to arrange the possible use of their fleet for the transportation of those that do not have access at the time to personal transportation.

iii. Maps - Good quality maps at an appropriate scale should be included in a few copies of this plan held by key individuals such as the EPC, Police Chief and transportation representative. Otherwise, reproductions may be used in other copies of the plan. Poster-size versions should be mounted or available in the EOC. A very suggestion which works ideally in these situations is to have the following routes superimposed onto aerial photographs of the area.

- **Major Transportation Routes** - This is intended to show the arteries for moving in and around the community so that alternate routes can be identified if need be.
- **Designated Evacuation Routes** - This will show the designated evacuation routes out of various parts of the community. These would be used by the police to block conflicting traffic in order to expedite efficient egress from affected areas.

4. Emergency Telecommunications Plan - The fourth of the common priority plans, the Emergency Telecommunications Plan ensures a means of communication between critical locations with a number of increasingly rudimentary communications options.

  a. Purpose - The purpose of the plan is to provide uninterrupted communications between vital points within the community and to points outside the community as needed during all phases of an emergency.

  b. Annual Review - This annual review, unlike most other emergency plans, has a large technical component that can rapidly be rendered obsolete. Therefore, in addition to annually reviewing policies and contact information, the telecommunications network must be reviewed for changes, enhancements or malfunctions, taking into consideration the number of lines, frequencies used and the number of radio/telephone/data units.

  c. Scope - As with all the plans mentioned in this book, the scale of application of this plan should be broad. This plan provides for effective communications via the highest means possible and reverts to increasingly simpler means as circumstances dictate. Its anticipatory back-up aspect would see it quietly put into use to ensure an alternate system is ready at all times.

d. **Concept of Operation** - The plan should provide for a number of communication options within the community which are available at all times for use as the circumstances dictates. It should also provide for communications with the next higher level of government that will provide the extraordinary support when the local government is overwhelmed.

e. **Objectives** - A number of simple objectives should be stated such as to have sufficient alternate communications means in preparation for any eventuality, anticipate the communications needs before they need arises, and to establish a common frequency and the attendant network control for inter-service communications.

f. **Activation** - Activation procedure for this plan should be at the discretion of the EPC after consultation with the Emergency Telecommunications Officer. The service provided by this plan is meant to be a seamless transition to alternate means when one fails so in order to be able to anticipate this need the plan must be deployed in tandem with the Emergency Management Plan.

g. **Callout Procedure** - Once contacted by the EPC, the call-out procedure lies with the Emergency Telecommunications Officer. He/she may contact the number of Amateur Radio operators as may be needed to fulfil the need and to cover the required locations.

h. **Telecommunications Officer** - The Telecommunications Officer is the central figure in the success of this plan. Ideally he/she will have the balance of technical knowledge of telecommunications systems, managerial skill to prepare and execute this plan, and foresight and intuition to anticipate the telecommunications needs of the EOC.

i. **Duties** - The basic duties should include: creating, exercising and reviewing this plan; establishing an alternate means of communication for any particular system currently in use by the EOC at any given time; recruiting and training a sufficient number of volunteers; consulting with the EOC and the EPC on telecommunication technical matters; and, maintaining a log of all communications his/her operators are responsible for.

ii. Immediate Action Checklist - An immediate action checklist should be detailed as a quick reference reminder of the important items that must be executed immediately upon being notified of an emergency and the deployment of the EOC. This is up to the Officer and will contain items specific to the jurisdiction and that local government.

i. Communications Room - The communications room is attached to the EOC and may take on a range of forms and degrees of importance. This will be determined in consultation with the EPC and the Chief Administrative Officer who will identify the role envisioned for the communications room (see message handling model).

i. Set-up - A specific layout of the communications room should be included. This details where the various pieces of equipment go and how information will flow into and out of the room. If not a permanently dedicated room, the location of pre-wired connections should be noted for easy location.

ii. Equipment - A complete equipment list should be included outlining everything needed to activate, operate and sustain the variety of telecommunications systems. This equipment may be permanently installed in a dedicated communications room or secured in a cabinet in or close to the designated room.

iii. Message Handling Model - See the text for a discussion of two common models. The model chosen should be set out here in the plan in different levels of detail depending upon the one chosen. This would involve a great deal of detail if all messages will pass through the communications room, or relatively little detail if the communications room is essentially a standby room to utilize Amateur Radio.

iv. Logs - Regardless of the model chosen, all messages passing through the communications room must be logged. A reproducible sample log sheet should be included and a large number of copies stored with the equipment.

v. Volunteers - Volunteers are the backbone of an emergency telecommunications system. The Officer must recruit a sufficient number of volunteers to staff the various locations required and to replace these with relief staff for prolonged operations. Volunteers must be properly trained and test via exercises.

vi. Hierarchy of Use - This section outlines the hierarchy of use of the various telecommunications systems that are commonly available. The systems available may vary from community to community. Generally, this would evolved from landline telephone, cellular telephone, facsimile, e-mail, pager and repeater-based radio systems to simplex radio (with or without power). The final level of communications is via runner who can make use of appropriate vehicles (snowmobile, boat, etc.)

viii. Service Protocol - The Officer, in association with the EPC, must reconcile how the EOC will function in terms of supporting the incident and possibly directing field resources vis a vis the role of the specific emergency service dispatch centres. This could take on a number of forms possibly including the EOC having absolute and immediate control over all field resources, or the emergency service representative in the EOC acting as an advisory only to the

Chief Administrative Officer and relaying department-specific directions back to his/her respective dispatch centre. Whatever the model, how this will be resolved should be clearly stated.

j. Staffing Remote Locations - Certain remote locations within or outside of the local government jurisdiction may have to be staffed by communicators for various reasons (i.e. dike patrol or to monitor reservoir levels). The plan should specifically note these locations and identify how the communicator will be delivered and how he/she will be relieved. Communication links should be tested to ensure contact is possible and an alternate system put in place (i.e. telephone and radio).

k. Prolonged Operations - As long as the EOC is deployed in support of an emergency, there should always be an alternate means of communication on standby for seamless transition. Therefore, the prolonged operations of the EOC are matched by the prolonged operations of the emergency telecommunications staff. The Officer must prepare for such by recruiting a sufficient number of volunteers to cover all necessary positions twenty-four hours per day for as long as is necessary.

l. Appendices

i. Network Diagram - A network diagram is an important graphical reference for picturing the entire telecommunications system of the local government. It shows the various interconnections, capabilities and capacities of the various sites of interest. For example, this would include the local government office, fire halls, the police station, hospital, water treatment plant, etc. This block diagram then relates the communication options for each site with the result being inconsistencies and vulnerabilities being identified. Conversely, strengths may emerge that may assist in planning the hierarchy of alternate communications means and identifying a common radio frequency.

ii. **Frequencies** - While these should be shown on the network diagram where applicable, a separate listing of radio frequencies should be kept for quick reference. This would be beneficial where the programming of radios is involved.

iii. **Volunteer Contact Information** - Like all other plans, an up-to-date and accurate listing of the names and telephone numbers of volunteers to be employed under this plan should be kept. In this case, it should include a large number of the local licensed Amateur Radio Operators, perhaps contact information for the local Amateur Radio club, other such trained volunteers and interested parties with the skills necessary for the plan to function smoothly.

C. **Hazard-Specific Preparedness Plans** - Hazard-specific preparedness plans cover the range of hazards identified earlier under Mitigation. As will have been noted by now, each plan has common "introductory" headings that cover necessary basics. The same is true for the range of hazard-specific preparedness plans. In addition, this range of plans has additional elements common to this type of plan which should be addressed in relation to the particular type of emergency envisioned. Ultimately, however, each hazard-specific preparedness plan must deal fully and completely with the type of impact envisioned by the hazard. Of necessity this will entail the addition of specific headings, information and resource listings. Such plans are prepared by experts in the particular hazard type (i.e. fire, civil unrest, mass casualty, infrastructure-related).

1. **Purpose** - In general terms, the purpose of a hazard-specific preparedness plan is to prepare the community for the impact of that threat and to anticipate the response needs.

2. **Annual Review** - The policies and procedures should be revisited annually to ensure their continued accuracy, relevance and efficacy. Also, ongoing mitigation efforts may change the nature of the specific threat necessitating changes in the anticipated response.

3. **Scope** - The principle from this book is that all such plans should be applicable over a range of impact scales. Thus, the plan could see use in small versions of the particular emergency being planned for right up to very large emergencies (i.e. flooding or landslides). Some hazards, however, may not have the luxury of scale and impact in a very significant manner when they happen (i.e. certain public health emergencies).

4. **Concept of Operation** - The concept of operation will set out how the need for the deployment of this plan will come about and how it will fulfil its purpose. The emergency services will respond to routine incidents. When the particular hazard is involved to a scale requiring centralized support, the Emergency Management Plan and the hazard-specific plan are called into use. As events escalate, this section would propose how greater use of specific resources would be employed.

5. **Objectives** - Objectives will be the benchmark against which the success of the plan will be measured. The objectives will vary with the desired use and efficacy of the particular plan. Nevertheless, they should be performance-oriented and related to fulfilling the purpose of the plan.

6. **Activation** - The actual activation of a hazard-specific plan will vary with the type of the emergency expected, the degree of urgency in its deployment and the extent of inconvenience, cost or restriction it entails. Some plans will be immediately called into use at the discretion of the Incident Commander, others may be authorized by the EPC, and other will be reserved for the approval of the Chief Administrative Officer.

7. **Threat Assessment** - This section should reiterate the assessment undertaken for this particular hazard in the Risk Assessment portion of the Mitigation section. Doing so indicates in the hazard-specific plan that a careful and thorough assessment of the threat posed by the particular hazard has been undertaken and incorporated in the preparedness provisions of this particular plan.

8. **Mitigation Efforts** - As above, this section would incorporate the Risk Management activities undertaken in the Mitigation section as they pertain to this particular hazard. Outlining what mitigation efforts have been taken will help the reader develop the proper frame of reference for viewing and assessing this hazard by

indicating what steps have been taken where they may not be obvious.

9. **Initial Response** - Articulating how the initial response may unfold will help prepare users of the plan for the early stages of its use. This is particularly important where the likely first agency on the scene may not be the one with the specific expertise. The issues attendant with such a situation should be identified and procedures developed to bridge the time until the experts arrive.

10. **Initial Action Checklist** - As a result of the scenario identified above, and even for situations where the emergency service with the specific expertise id the first to arrive, an immediate action checklist is recommended. This serves two purposes: it provides the memory aid to the responder so that important steps are not overlooked, and it provides a guide to the EOC staff as to what will be, or what was retrospectively, the steps that will/were taken in the initial stages.

11. **Multiple Agency Integration** - As a result of an escalating emergency or one that starts off immediately as a multiple-jurisdictional emergency, the integration of these into the response process must be anticipated. This is greatly expedited by wide application of the Incident Command System.

12. **Prolonged Operations** - Largely determined by the type and extent of the emergency, preparations for prolonged operations should be made. This involves relief staff, back-up equipment for items becoming unserviceable or items consumed, and the support (e.g. food and water) for staff while executing their duties. This may be the calling of off-duty staff or providing for such via a mutual aid agreement with a neighbouring local government.

13. **Security** - In some instances security of a scene may be necessary for a number of reasons, foremost of which is public safety. Where evacuations are ordered, security issues can be combined with provisions under the Evacuation Plan.

14. **Demobilization** - Incidents don't simply just stop; Instead there is a release of resources as the particular situation is addressed. The hazard-specific preparedness plan should anticipate this need and allow for resupply, restocking or repair of resources consumed.

15. **Appendices**
    a. **Additional Resources** - Where it is believed that unique or extraordinary volumes of resources will be

required, this should be provided for in an appendix. The contact person, telephone number and location of the resources should be noted. If a mutual aid agreement is involved, it should be included here or a specific reference made to it if it is in the Mutual Aid appendix of the Emergency Management Plan.

b. Contact Information (including Alternates) - The name and telephone number of key personnel to the execution of this plan should be included and verified on a regular basis. Include secondary and tertiary alternates as well.

III. Recovery Plans - Local governments must plan for what comes after the response to an emergency. Lives have been saved and catastrophe avoided but the ability of the local government to execute all of its functions has been impaired and facilities have been damaged. Foresight would dictate that recovery plans are a necessity.

A. Service Continuation Plan - The Service Continuation Plan in indispensable. This will ensure that important business functions and key services are maintained or restored in priority.

1. Purpose - The purpose of this plan is to identify vulnerabilities in local government business and service delivery functions and plan for devastating impact by hazards facing the community.

2. Annual Review - Annual review is particularly important with this plan and the reasons why should be noted. Local government operations are complex and broad in scope and application. These change regularly in response to the demands of the community and the financial ability of the local government to pay for them. Some are long-standing services while others are fleeting: some are certainly less important than others. An annual review to assess these will ensure the truly important functions and services are addressed.

3. Scope - The scope of this plan is different from the other plans. It plans for the worst case scenario and therefore anticipates taking drastic remedial action to restore a service or maintain a function. Although some elements of the plan can be used in various minor disruptions or in planned interruptions, the actions generally called for are in the plan might be too extreme. However, under certain circumstances one function or service identified under the plan may be devastated while others are largely unaffected. The plan can be brought to bear in its full capacity on the one aspect if called for. This is the one plan that generally is saved for "the big one" simply by virtue of it inherent nature.

4. **Concept of Operation** - This plan requires the input of the staff providing the particular critical service of function. It should, therefore, be an important part of each division or section of the local government's business operations. As such, it gets called into play as and when needed by the affected groups (see activation).

5. **Objectives** - The objectives result from the Service Impact Analysis which determines recovery times under the Maximum Tolerable Disruption Time. Those important time objectives may be included here.

6. **Activation** - Depending on the extent of the recovery measures required, activation of portions of the plan as it applies to certain parts of the local government may be at the discretion of the section/ division/department head. If extreme measures are the course of action or if the impact has affected the entire spectrum of local government services and functions, higher level authorization for activation may necessary. This should rest with the Chief Administrative Officer.

7. **Basic Assumptions** - In planning for the worst case scenario, certain basic assumptions will be made. These should be specified. These might include such things as widespread power failure, building uninhabitable, key person not being available, etc.

8. **Service Impact Analysis** - This analysis is an enterprise-wide project that reviews all services and functions of the local government. This task is best executed through the use of standardized forms circulated to each section or division of the local government who identify their respective services and functions, and prioritize each using the PHTO Model outlined in the text.

   a. **Critical Service Functions** - Certain critical services and functions will emerge from the analysis. These are arrived at by assessing the risk exposure of each. Certain critical services may be highly sheltered from risk while other contributory routine support services may not. The local government must consider the interconnections between services to ensure the necessary support elements for the really critical services are there when needed.

b. Risk Assessment - see above.

c. Critical Service Function Priorities and Objectives - Using a form such as the one shown in the text, critical services can be ranked and a score attached. This assists in determining priorities as well as deriving the service-specific return-to-operation time objective.

9. Initial Response - This section is linked to the basic assumptions mentioned earlier. It should articulate what the initial response should be upon the devastating impact of an emergency. It should involve how the extent of the emergency will be assessed, who will determine what is salvageable, how the transition will to alternate measures will take place and how will staff be informed.

a. Alternate Processing Systems (Manual Systems) - If manual systems are to be used as a temporary measure, these should be specifically identified and the location of supplies for their use noted. Any specific instructions on how these manual systems are to be operated or any special rules should be included.

b. Alternate Site - An alternate site is prudent. Its location, setup, operation and how the order to move to it will be given should be addressed here.

c. Immediate Action Checklists - As with the other immediate action checklists noted throughout this book, this serves as a memory aid to key individuals. In this case such checklists should be provided for section or division heads who will have specific (and generally common) steps to take in assessing the situation, taking the necessary remedial steps and informing the EOC or EPC.

d. Back-up Computing - This has two elements: emergency computer supplies (including hardware and software) and backup data. Where hardware or software have been damaged, rapid replacement is important. Once these are restored to basic operating capacities, data must be provided. A fundamental policy for backup off-site data storage must be developed and followed.

e. Equipment Suppliers - A list of reliable suppliers of all supplies and equipment used in, and consumed by, a particular office should be listed. Delivery time may be critical, so discussions in the planning stage with suppliers should address their ability to provide important elements quickly, e.g., computer servers, software, etc.)

10. **Restoration of Service Level** - Returning to normal service levels is a considerable process outlined in the text. Here much more immediate and practical matters are considered with the following points being two of potentially many.

   a. **Entering Manual Records** - If manual systems have been used, those records will have to be put into the regular systems once those are again operational. This section should provide for how, when and by whom this will be done.

   b. **New Equipment** - It is inevitable that some equipment will need to be replaced. This section should contemplate how appropriate equipment will be selected and what factors may affect its delivery, installation and commissioning.

11. **Appendices**

   a. **Suppliers' Contact Information** - This is related to equipment suppliers discussed above. Such a list should be comprehensive so that any supplies, hardware or software required can be easily located.

   b. **Staff Contact Information** (to include alternates) - An accurate and up-to-date staff telephone contact list must be maintained. It should include alternates.

B. **Facilities Inspection and Repair Plan** - Like the Service Continuation Plan, the Facilities Inspection and Repair Plan is an important part of recovery. Recognizing that recovery is a long-term process, facilities will need to be assessed in the immediate post-emergency period and their repair planned for.

   1. **Purpose** - The purpose of the plan is to provide for a system of evaluation of local government facilities and their repair, where needed, after an emergency.

   2. **Annual Review** - Things change more slowly when planning for the built environment but an annual review of this plan should be undertaken to be consistent with the message of regularly reviewing all plans. Issues for consideration include new construction, changes in use or changes in the physical plant of any facility.

3. **Scope** - This plan is intended to address a significant emergency affecting a number of local government facilities. It will find application in more limited scale emergencies affecting one or a few facilities such as a blast in or around a building, or a fire.

4. **Concept of Operation** - This plan is employed in the post-emergency phase. It uses skilled staff members, volunteers or paid professionals to conduct the assessments. The extent of coordination will depend on the number of local government facilities and their degree of separation.

5. **Objectives** - Objectives should be time-oriented and address two areas: the inspection of facilities and then their return to service.

6. **Activation** - This plan could have two type of activation: if buildings are prioritized, the inspection and assessment could begin immediately after the emergency by the assigned inspector; or, if the EOC waits to see how an emergency develops, it can activate the plan and send inspectors in to the affected areas.

7. **Deemed Qualified Professionals** - Potentially a large numbers of qualified inspectors may be needed. The plan should provide for Building Inspectors, Architects and Engineers to be authorized to undertake inspections.

8. **Post-Emergency Evaluation** - The text notes a triage-like system of evaluation that should be reiterated here in the plan for the benefit of plan users.

   a. **Rapid Evaluation** - This is a quick visual assessment of the obvious structural members.

   b. **Detailed Evaluation** - This involves a more detailed walkthrough of damaged buildings assessing less obvious structural components.

   c. **Engineering Evaluation** - A very thorough assessment using supporting documents such as plans and structural calculations.

9. **Post-Inspection Classification** - Once inspected buildings are given one of three designations

which should be stated so users of the plan know the system employed.

a. Inspected - building is safe to enter.

b. Limited Entry - building is not safe but safe enough for limited entry by certain authorized persons.

c. Unsafe - unsafe for entry.

10. **Non-Structural Hazards** - This section simply serves as a reminder to users of the plan that non-structural elements of buildings, such as glazing, parapets and mechanical systems, also pose serious hazards.

11. **Essential Facilities** - Certain local government facilities may be given priority treatment by being designated an essential facility.

a. Designated - Such facilities should be specifically named.

b. Facility Plans - In planning for a post-emergency evaluation, copies of all relevant facility plans and documents should be gathered.

c. Designated Inspectors - An inspector and alternates should be designated for each facility. This may be staff plant engineers or an appropriate professional residing or working in the general vicinity.

d. Pre-Emergency Inspection and Familiarization - The designated inspector and the alternates should become intimately familiar with important aspects of the facility in question. Familiarization would include a detailed review of the documents gathered above.

12. **Repair Planning** - A plan for repairing the facility would have to be developed after the post-emergency inspection. Certain vulnerable components can be anticipated to be affected in an emergency.

a. Fixed Equipment Inventory - An inventory of fixed equipment should be kept for repair and replacement purposes. This would include make, model number and any other technical operating information pertinent to its repair.

13. Appendices

a. Contact Information and Alternates - This need to be maintained accurately and to be up-to-date. Periodic checks of the list under telephone fan-out exercise are useful.

b. Inspectors - A list of deemed qualified inspectors should be kept with their address and telephone number if not included above. Note any cases where an inspector is assigned an essential facility.

c. Major Equipment Suppliers - Keep a list of suppliers for the types of major components that may need replacing. This may include air conditioners, uninterrupted power supplies, compressors, turbine parts, etc.

d. Specialty Resources - Provided for anything not captured under the above.

APPENDIX B:

SAMPLE SERVICE IMPACT ANALYSIS DOCUMENTS

Service Impact Analysis:
Critical Service Function Objectives and Strategies

Service Function: (name of service provided)

_____

_____

Scenario: (describe scenario affecting service delivery - use separate sheets for multiple scenarios)

_____

_____

_____

Ranking:

Impact of Scenario Occurring

Maximum Tolerable Disruption
Time for this Service

	Low	Medium	High
High	2	3	3
Medium	1	2	3
Low	1	1	2

Probability of Scenario Occurring

Maximum Tolerable Disruption Time for this Service	
< 1 to 1 day	5
2 to 4 days	4
5 to 7 days	3
8 to 10 days	2
> 10 days	1

probability/impact value = _____   X   MTDT value _____ =

score _____

(mark appropriate box "x" and enter value)   (select MTDT and enter value)   (high

score=high priority)

Business Impact (Quantitative and/or Qualitative): (describe the likely impact of the scenario on the delivery of this service)

_____

_____

_____

Return to Operation Objective(s): (when should all or part of this service be returned to operation - relates to MTDT)

_____

_____
_____
_____

Proactive Strategy: (describe the strategy to avoid this scenario from occurring)

_____
_____
_____
_____
_____

____

Reactive Strategy: (describe the strategy to be employed if this scenario does occur)

_____
_____
_____
_____

_____

Recovery Steps: (list the steps to achieve the RTO objective(s) - incorporate the reactive strategy)

_____
_____
_____
_____

_____

Key Person(s): (name the person(s) involved in the delivery of this service)

_____

_____

Input (records, data, information): (what input, if any, is required to perform this service)

_____
_____
_____

_____

Processing Systems (forms, hardware, software): (what systems are used to deliver this service)

_____
_____
_____

_____

Suppliers (and alternates) of Input and Processing Systems: (name the suppliers of the processing systems and one alternate supplier)

_____
_____
_____

_____

Linkages to Other Service Functions (specify): (does this service affect/interact with any other services of the corporation)

_____

_____

Sample "Likely Scenarios" Matrix for Service Continuation Planning

		Likely Scenarios			
		Office not Habitable	Computer-Based	Staff	Other

Appendix B: Sample Service Impact analysis Documents

Function	Responsible Staff	Fire	Water Damage	Structural Damage	Biological	Mechanical	Gas Leak	Theft of Hardware	Data Corrupted (Hacker/Virus)	Software Corrupted (Hacker/Virus)	Software Failure	Hardware Failure	Data Lines Corrupted	Loss of Key Personnel	Catastrophic Human Error	Labour Dispute	Severe Winter Storm	Telecommunications Failure	Prolonged Power Outage	Theft of Critical Documents
Financial																				
Payroll	Sally																			
Accounts Payable	Mary																			
Accounts Receivable	Donna																			
Transmission of Taxes	Sally																			
General Ledger Maintenance	Sally																			
Records																				
Minutes	Dave																			
Legal Plans	Donna																			
Bylaws/Ordinances	Dave																			
Certificates of Title	Donna																			
Insurance Documents	Donna																			
Permits	Bob																			
Warranties	Donna																			
P.W. Plans/Schematics	Rod																			
Continuity of Governance																				
Meeting Place	Dave																			
Agenda Building	Dave																			
Processing Correspondence	Dave																			
Processing of Bylaws	Bob																			
Approval of Cheque Register	Dave																			
Services																				
Cemetery Plot Sales	Mary																			
Garbage Collection	Rod																			
Business Licenses	Sally																			
Dog Licenses	Sally																			
Building Permits & Advice	Sally																			
Planning Advice &Approvals	Ralph																			
Bylaw Enforcement	Bob																			
Subdivision Approval	Bob																			
Information Requests	Bob																			
Web Page	Bob																			
P.W. Alarm System	Rod																			

APPENDIX C:

SAMPLE TRAINING MATRIX

Sample Emergency Program Training Matrix

	Chief Admin. Officer	Senior Managers	Emerg. Prog. Coordinator	Deputy EPC	Fire Chief	Deputy Fire Chief	Fire Officers	Firefighters	Police Chief	Deputy Police Chief	Police Officers	Ambulance Chief	Deputy Ambulance Chief	Emergency Medical Techs.	Public Works Manger	Deputy Public Works Mgr.	P. W. Crewmembers	Hospital Administrator	Deputy Hospital Admin.	Senior Hospital Managers	ESS Director	Deputy ESS Director	ESS Staff	Telecomm. Officer	Deputy Telecomm. Officer	Radio Operators	Public Information Officer	Public Information Clerk			
Intro. to Emerg. Planning																															
Basic Emerg. Management																															
Hazard/Risk Analysis																															
Preparedness Planning																															
Response Planning																															
Recovery Planning																															
Mitigation Planning																															
EOC Implementation																															
EOC Operations																															
Emergency Evacuations																															
Intro. to Emerg. Exercises																															
Tabletop Exercises																															
Functional & Full-scale Exercises																															
Public Information																															
Emerg. Telecomms.																															
Intro. to ICS																															
Basic ICS																															
Intermediate ICS																															
Advanced ICS																															
Introduction to ESS																															
Reception Center ps.																															
ESS Reg/Inq./Referral																															
ESS Admin Support																															
Group Lodging Ops.																															
ESS Component Services																															
ESS Resource Acquisition																															
Managing Walk-in Volunteers																															
ESS Leadership																															
ESS Director																															

APPENDIX D:

THE PROFESSIONAL EMERGENCY MANAGER

This book is intended to be used and relied upon by the local government staff member assigned the responsibility of the Emergency Program Coordinator. In keeping with the philosophy that the Comprehensive Emergency Management Plan can and should be created locally and within the limited resources of small- to medium-sized local governments, it is expected that this person will be a full-time employee with primary responsibilities in another area of local government management and not a full-time professional emergency management professional.

It is worth noting, however, that professional emergency managers do exist and that training and certification is available. These professionals are employed by all levels of government and the private sector as full-time employees, or as consultants on an as-needed basis. This appendix will offer a brief discussion of what training is available, the different certifications available and retaining a professional emergency manager.

EMERGENCY MANAGEMENT EDUCATION

Emergency management education is a vast topic with a form of self-directed or formal education to meet virtually every need and in every facet of this broad subject area.

This book is a prime example of the self-help guides. Many books have been written on the different aspects of emergency management and some have been so bold as to attempt comprehensive treatment of the subject. In some cases, as this book has attempted to portray, such "how-to" reference manuals may be the complete course in emergency management required by the full-time employee but part-time Emergency Program Coordinator in a small local government.

Beyond this, the ambitious Emergency Program Coordinator may wish to pursue formal education. Formal education may include continuing professional development courses through professional bodies; courses offered by industry groups; courses or programs offered by state or national emergency planning/training bodies and institutes; or, credit courses offered by a recognized educational institution. This spectrum of availability is matched by the variety of subjects on every aspect of emergency planning, management and response. This gives the student a significant choice in how involved they wish to get in seeking formal education in this field.

Courses and programs sponsored by professional organizations, industry groups and state or national bodies and institutes are difficult to track, and hence comment on, as they are either regional in nature or offered sporadically. Experience has shown that these courses are of an extremely practical nature by being either regionally relevant when based on certain hazards or types of management systems, or when they are based on certain industry or interest group areas of expertise, e.g., mitigation from the insurance perspective or mass casualty emergency medicine.

It appears that most states, provinces and regional associations of small national governments, e.g. the Caribbean and Southeast Asia, have some form of training institute that would make it too large of a field to cover in this section. The Emergency Program Coordinator looking for training from such bodies would be best served by asking or researching locally for what organization will be offering which courses and when.

From observing this field for many years, it is apparent that the number of formal educational institutions offering courses in this area expands and contracts as niches are found or lost for various individual programs. A general observation, though, would note that programs are being added as our society in general places increasing emphasis on formal education.

The Natural Hazards Research and Applications Information Center at the University of Colorado has assembled the most comprehensive international listing of recognized educational institutions offering courses in emergency/hazard/disaster management. This listing identifies fifty-nine institutions offering one or more courses in some aspect of emergency management, thirty-nine offering certificate programs, concentrations and minors, seventeen offering Associate Degree programs, nineteen offering Bachelor Degree programs, and thirty-five offering graduate degree programs.

The range of programs offered allows the individual considering formal education a host of options to meet one's specific needs. This may range from one course in a specific area to boost one's understanding of a particularly complex or important aspect of emergency management, to some level of recognized Degree that reflects a mastery of this very broad subject.

The large number of institutions offering programs will each have a specific focus or emphasis to the program. Anyone considering such programs should thoroughly investigate a range of schools to find one that meets the long-term goal of the student and is balanced against the practical considerations of full-time work/part-time student and affordability.

EMERGENCY MANAGEMENT CERTIFICATION

Current research reveals four internationally recognized emergency management certifications that practitioners may wish to pursue or employers may wish to consider as desirable qualifications. Whether these are pursued for personal reasons or as a condition of employment, certification as a professional emergency manager lends a great deal of credibility to one's position and professionalism as these certifications speak to a combination of experience, education, examination and, usually, continuing professional education. Each of these four certifications is briefly outlined below and in no order of recognition, preference or difficulty in achieving.

Disaster Recovery Institute International
This organization is concerned with business continuity planning and offer three levels of certification. These are Associate Business Continuity Professional (ABCP), Certified Business Continuity Professional (CBCP), and Master Business Continuity Professional (MBCP). There is a membership exam and a continuing education program requiring recertification every two years.

Business Continuity Institute
As the name implies, this organization is also focuses on business continuity planning. It has several membership categories with Fellow (FBCI) and Member (MBCI) being considered "statutory members" under British law while Associate, Companion, Affiliate and Student are considered "non-statutory members." Membership is granted based upon a scored assessment of information submitted by the applicant (to include experience and education). For admittance as a Fellow, an interview is required.

Certified Risk Managers International
Risk Management is the core concept of this organization which offers the Certified Risk Manager (CRM) designation. A comprehensive five subject/five exam program

qualifies one for membership while a continuing education program is required to maintain that membership.

International Association of Emergency Managers

This is the fourth of the major certifications and perhaps the most widely applicable to general emergency management. It offers the Certified Emergency Manager (CEM) designation for which the qualification requirements are a peer review of experience and education plus an exam. There is also a continuing education aspect to maintain the certification. Unique to this organization is an affiliation of state emergency management associations with their own entrance requirements. Most U.S. states appear to have such a chapter with some having their own professional designations. For example, Oklahoma has the Oklahoma Certified Emergency Manager while Florida has three levels of membership: Associate Emergency Manager, Professional Emergency Manager and Certified Emergency Manager. These associations have various entrance requirements but usually involve a local experience component.

Other Certifications

Two other certifications are worth noting. These are: Certified Crisis Operations Manager sponsored by the University of Richmond and Certified Recovery Planner sponsored by the Harris Disaster Recovery Institute. Both of these maintain rigorous entrance requirements through multiple exams.

Benefits of membership in these professional bodies vary but the identifiable core include peer and professional recognition, networking with others in the field, enhanced career opportunities, resource materials, periodicals and an annual convention/professional development institute. So organizations go so far as to offer liability insurance, health insurance, discounts with certain services and bulk purchasing power.

RETAINING A PROFESSIONAL EMERGENCY MANAGER

The philosophy of this book has been that within small to medium sized local governments, Comprehensive Emergency Management is generally attainable within existing staff levels and financial resources. There should not be a need to retain outside help to create a Comprehensive Emergency Management Plan that is to be an innate part of that local government.

It is recognized, however, that at times an outside consultant will need to be retained to write such a plan, supplement particularly important or complex aspects of such a plan as determined by local circumstances, or to assist in certain aspects of the overall emergency program, such as with training or exercise development/facilitation/monitoring.

The best guidelines to follow in this regard are those generally applied in any other aspect of local government contracting. Specifically, if it is the first time a consultant has been retained in a specific area of expertise, shop around to solicit interest. This is best done with a Request for Expressions of Interest or a Request for Proposal.

Expression of Interest is an advertisement outlining what the local government generally wished to achieve and asks for any interested firms to register themselves with the local government. This usually includes companies providing a profile of their staff and areas of experience as it pertains to the possible future project.

A *Request for Proposal* commences the legal tendering process that outlines a specific project and implies someone, not necessarily the lowest bidder if the request is worded adequately, will be awarded a contract by the local government. The local government is committed to a course of action under the common law and should only use this approach when it is certain of what it desires to achieve.

Both routes require advertising to solicit input. Wording should be very clear to avoid any needless input from unqualified firms which takes staff time to review. Tendering processes may vary according to local laws and local purchasing/contracting procedures, but in the case of such specialty services, wide circulation may be necessary especially in the smaller communities. In addition to local newspapers, wider circulated regional newspapers or those of the largest adjacent community should be used. As well, trade publications of regional/state/national emergency planning organizations or those of professional bodies should also be considered.

Notwithstanding local laws on the selection of bidders, the local government should consider experience in the specific area(s) desired rather than solely on cost. A general rule to follow is that experienced consultants do not come cheaply. This, however, must be balanced against over-priced consultants.

Once retained, ensure that any contract has specific objectives that are simple, measurable and achievable. Vague contracts that are open-ended are an unscrupulous consultant's dream. While the vast majority of consultants in this field are genuinely enthusiastic about helping clients achieve greater security through solid and competent emergency planning, it is still in the best interest of the local government as custodian of the public interest and public finances, to articulate a firm direction to any consultant and use objectives as a performance measurement.

While far from authoritative or exhaustive, this brief section should alert the Emergency Program Coordinator to what education is available if so desired, what types of certification are available and what they really imply, and things to consider if outside help is to be retained.

APPENDIX E:

EMERGENCY MANAGEMENT RESOURCES

The Internet has been a boon to all persons active in emergency management by enabling the proliferation of web sites that facilitate the rapid dissemination of information. A simple search on one's favorite search engine using phrases such as "emergency management," "emergency planning," "disaster recovery" or any specific type of hazard usually results in several hundreds, if not thousands, of responses. These responses will include everything from not-for-profit societies, government institutes or offices, consultants, educational institutes, interested individuals, links mistakenly indexed and disreputable links intentionally indexed.

It would be impractical, not to mention of questionable utility, to attempt a systematic review or survey of the innumerable sites in cyberspace. Instead, this appendix will simply identify the (few) most useful sites known to the author at the time of writing that are in keeping with the self-help theme of this book. Inevitably, some important web pages will be overlooked. Web pages not included here is no reflection of their content or presentation, rather, what is presented are a handful of sites where the Emergency Program Coordinator can find supporting material, or at least links onward to pursue that particular thread, for most topics covered in this book.

U.S. Federal Emergency Management Agency
http://www.fema.gov

All browsers will eventually point here. The Federal Emergency Management Agency of the U.S. Government is the powerhouse of on-line information and resources. Not only is it a source of U.S. government activities and policies, it is also a highly informative source for current events in this field as well as useful reference material for all levels of emergency management practitioner. A useful way to view the structure of the entire FEMA page which greatly aids in locating information is to select the *site index* button at the bottom of the main page. This then conveniently lists the web site contents alphabetically.

A useful service provided by FEMA is the Global Emergency Management System (GEMS) which is essentially their links page. What makes this so useful is the extensive listing of links and the ability to search the list. These links related to most aspects of emergency management.

In addition to forward links to other relevant sites, the most useful aspect of this site is the provision of specific information, such as documents, policies, procedures and checklists, that most emergency planners will find applicable.

Disaster! Finder
http://ltpwww.gsfc.nasa.gov/ndrd/disaster/links/

Disaster! Finder, also known as The Disaster Finder, is a service provided by NASA's Solid Earth and Natural Hazards Program. This is one of the best listings of emergency management information available on the web with over six hundred links. These links are grouped in an intuitive way that allows for easy research while a search function aids in locating useful information. Of the six main headings (Disaster Management, Disciplines, General, Organizations, Systems, Type), Disaster Management is the largest with extensive links relating to all aspects of Comprehensive Emergency Management. Also of interest is the listing of hazards by type. This covers a large number of possible emergencies that may be relevant to one's own community.

The type of information accessed through these links is quite varied in its usefulness but is certainly all-inclusive. Information ranges from further links to other agencies and organizations, to response summaries from past event, statistical information and actual self-help guides. Experience has shown this site to be of great benefit when researching specific information on particular hazards and in acquiring mitigation and preparedness details from other jurisdictions.

Natural Hazards Center at the University of Colorado, Boulder
http://wwwcolorado.edu/hazards

The Natural Hazards Center at the University of Colorado (Boulder) is another noticeable Internet powerhouse in this field. Being a premier academic institution, its information is heavily weighted towards academia although a great deal of the information provided is useful to the layman and generally relevant to local government emergency management.

The web site is very large so the search function expedites one's research. The index page breaks the site down into its constituent parts that include: an extensive on-line library database; information on periodical and listserve services provided as a means of staying current; a listing of publications the Center has produced that include working papers on ongoing research at the Center, Quick Response Reports that follow emergencies that have occurred, and a bibliography of U.S. natural hazards; and, a current list of outside publications in this field, other periodicals, organizations dedicated to hazard and disaster management, and upcoming conferences and training sessions.

This is an extremely useful site that local government emergency managers should become familiar with as it is a potential source for answers to most questions that may arise in hazard inventory, risk analysis and risk assessment.

Disaster Preparedness and Emergency Response Association
http://disasters.org

The Disaster Preparedness and Emergency Response Association (DERA) is a not-for profit organization founded in 1962 to assist communities world-wide in disaster preparedness, response and recovery, and to serve as a link for professionals, volunteers, and organizations active in all phases of emergency preparedness and management.

In order to achieve this objective, DERA has assembled a web site that would be quite helpful to anyone working in most areas of emergency management. Its opening page offers four useful services: its quarterly newsletter; internet links, a limited library of reference publications; and, Emergency Management Gold which is a separate site also with extensive Internet links.

The Internet links cover a wide range of useful topics including alerts and emergency information, special events, emergency management information resources, emergency management associations, emergency communications, news sources, and security and safety.

Canadian Center for Emergency Preparedness
http://www.ccep.ca

The Canadian Center for Emergency Preparedness is a not-for-profit organization dedicated to the promotion of emergency management. It has put together a good web site that touches on the important aspects of its objective that include: personal preparedness; education, training and certification; research and publications;

templates; and, links. Structuring the page in this intuitive manner makes it easy to use and to locate the desired information.

The strength of this site is the number of highly relevant local government related documents. For example, it is one of the few sites that has documentation on neighbourhood-level emergency planning with information on Community Emergency Response Teams (CERT) and Strengthening Preparedness Among Neighbors (SPAN). The site also has very useful templates that may be downloaded and used as a guide in developing different types of plans. Several examples of different types of plans are also offered. Finally, the site also provides links to many local government web pages that have information on their respective emergency programs. These in turn offer differing degrees of information with some being quite useful through the inclusion of their emergency plan. When one is researching or compiling a plan, such web pages can be a great source of insight into how other communities have addressed certain planning issues.

Emergency Preparedness Information Exchange
http://epix.hazard.net/index.html

The Emergency Preparedness Information Exchange, known as EPIX, is hosted at Simon Fraser University in British Columbia. It is a simple site whose greatest contribution is a detailed listing of, and links to, international emergency planning organizations. Those looking for information from other areas of the world affected by a certain hazard, such as wildfires in Australia or floods in the U.K., may find these links of assistance.

The site also offers a "Topics" page which has links to organizations dedicated to certain aspects of emergency management and includes a few reports or planning guides on selected hazards in PDF format.

Emergency Management Australia
http://ema.gov.au

Emergency Management Australia is the federal agency responsible for reducing the impact of natural and human-caused disasters on the Australian community. It is also the lead agency for coordinating federal disaster response on that continent. Consequently, the web site of EMA is a mixture of federal policy that facilitates its mandate and self-help information targeted at citizens, schools and their communities.

The Community Safety section of the web page contains information of most interest to local government emergency planners. This includes a good overview of a number of natural and human-caused hazards faced by Australian communities as well as preparedness and response information for individuals and households. The site also includes the on-line version of a very useful 48 page booklet entitled "Hazards, Disasters and Survival" designed for students and members of the community.

Asian Disaster Preparedness Center
http://www.adpc.ait.ac.th

As the name implies, this Center's focus is specific to Asia, and Southeast Asia in particular. The Asian Disaster Preparedness Center is based at the Asian Institute of Technology in Bangkok and is the regional resource center dedicated to "disaster reduction for safer communities and sustainable development."

Its primary benefit would be to emergency managers working in this part of the world as the Center seems to be the leader in training, information dissemination and mitigation projects for this area. The site offers discussion forums and newsletters as well as research, extensive education programs and technical assistance.

Of particular interest to local government emergency planners or non-governmental organizations in the region would be the Asian Urban Disaster Mitigation Program which was launched in 1995. This is ADPC's largest program, operating in eight nations, and was designed to make cities safer from disasters with the goal of reducing the disaster vulnerability of urban populations, infrastructure, critical facilities and shelter in targeted cities. Professional training is a critical part of this program.

The site also contains a comprehensive list of emergency management web sites in the region as well as a good list of international sites.

Disaster Relief
http://www.disasterrelief.org

Disaster Relief is a cooperative effort of the American Red Cross, CNN Interactive and IBM. Its mission is to help disaster victims and the disaster relief community world-wide by facilitating the exchange of information on the Internet.

It appears that the consortium has achieved a balance of international, national and local level information dissemination. Its links page has an impressive range of links covering most relevant topics at a range of scales including international-level natural hazard and aid organizations down to state-level emergency planning offices. Its library has a large number of brochures and pamphlets in several formats and languages for a host of possible emergencies ranging from residential fires to heat waves. It is this list of brochures and pamphlets that will interest the local government emergency planner as this self-help information is geared for individuals and families.

Global Disaster Information Network
http://www.gdin-international.org

The Global Disaster Information Network (GDIN) is a recent innovation that emerged from the frustration of persons working in this field around the world to locate and share relevant information that is in useful formats. The aim of GDIN is to provide the right information, in the right format, to the right people, in time to make the right decisions.

The links page has connections to several good documents on specific hazards, such as hurricanes and flooding, but otherwise is quite limited. This site has tremendous potential but in its infancy it is of limited utility to local government emergency planners.

Rothstein Associates Inc. and The Rothstein Catalog On Disaster Recovery
http://www.rothstein.com

Rothstein Associates Inc. is a consulting firm based in Connecticut specializing in business continuity management, crisis management, disaster avoidance and risk assessment. A very successful component of this operation is the Rothstein Catalog on Disaster Recovery which has emerged as the industry's leading source for 1,000+ books, software tools, research reports and videos. This on-line catalogue is an extensive listing of relevant publications covering most areas of emergency management. This should be the site of preference for the emergency manager when looking to purchase reference materials.

The company's web page is also a source for detailed information on business continuity planning and service level agreements with feature articles, a discussion forum and the Business Survival Newsletter.

Finally, this site has an extensive list of links to sites covering a broad range of emergency management topics, including information technology, the Incident Command System and natural hazards.

REFERENCES

Applied Technology Council of California. 1989. Procedures for Post-Earthquake Safety Evaluation of Buildings.

B.C. Ministry of Finance and Corporate Relations. 1992. Business Continuation Planning.

British Columbia Ministry of Forests. 1990. S-411 Risk Management.

Burbridge, J. 1989. *Is Your Organization Ready For A Disaster?* Emergency Preparedness Digest. Jul-Sep.

Burns, E. 1994. *Surviving a Disaster Takes a Plan, Not a Miracle!* Disaster Recovery Journal. Jul/Aug/Sep.

Hussong, W.A. 1994. *So You're the Company's New Contingency Planner!* Disaster Recovery Journal. Jan/Feb/Mar.

Inter-Agency Emergency Preparedness Committee. Undated. A Discussion Paper for an Emergency Management System for British Columbia Based on the Incident Command System Principles.

Justice Institute of British Columbia. 1993. A Guide to the New Emergency Program Act.

Justice Institute of British Columbia. 1995. The Need For Exercises and Types of Exercises. Unpublished handout.

Justice Institute of British Columbia. 1997. Exercise Process course manual.

Laughy, L. 1990. <u>A Planner's Handbook for Emergency Preparedness</u>. Vancouver: UBC Center for Human Settlements.

Lawson, R. 2000. *Exercising Business Continuation Plans Without Training and Exercise, Your Plan is Wasted*. Municipal Insurance Association Newsletter <u>Exchange</u>. May.

Major Industrial Accidents Council of Canada. 1996. <u>Basic Risk Assessment Course</u>.

Mitchell, J. 1983. *When Disaster Strikes... The Critical Incident Stress Debriefing Process*. <u>Journal of Emergency Medical Services</u>. Vol. 8.

Perry, L.G. 1994. *Preparing for an Emergency: A Step-by-Step Approach*. <u>Disaster Recovery Journal</u>. Oct/Nov/Dec.

Province of British Columbia. 1996. <u>Emergency Program Act</u>, RSBC 1996, Ch. 111.

Wilson, B. 1988. *City of Edmonton: An Emergency Plan That Works*. <u>Emergency Preparedness Digest</u>. July/Sept.

Wold, G.H. 1992. *The Disaster Recovery Planning Process*. <u>Disaster Recovery Journal</u>. Jan/Feb/Mar.

Wold, G.H., and Shriver, R.F. 1993. *Selecting Business Recovery Strategies*. <u>Disaster Recovery Journal</u>. Jul/Aug/Sep.

GLOSSARY

Activation is a section of the Emergency Management Plan that details how the Comprehensive Emergency Management Plan is called into use. This involves a designated person, usually the Emergency Program Coordinator, assessing such a request or developing scenario and determining whether at all, or a full or partial deployment of the Emergency Operations Center, and hence use of the Plan, is justified.

Amateur Radio is a service of volunteer radio operators who have met minimum technical and operating skills necessary for obtaining a Federally issued license. Amateur Radio operators, also known as "Hams" or Ham Radio Operators, exist in most communities and may be recruited for the purpose of providing reliable emergency communications.

All Hazards Approach is a philosophy of including all potential hazards facing a community in the Risk Assessment portion of the Mitigation exercise.

Call Center is a combination of an established telephone number available to be called for information on an emergency and the facilities and staff to answer the telephone calls. It is established as part of the Emergency Public Information Plan and will involve a multi-line telephone system.

Chief Administrative Officer is the senior non-elected public servant in a local government. This position may also be known as Administrator, City Manager, Clerk, Commissioner, etc.

Comprehensive Emergency Management is the concept which ensures that all aspects of anticipating, minimizing the risks from, preparing for and recovering from, an emergency are systematically addressed. It consists of four phases: mitigation, preparedness, response and recovery.

Comprehensive Emergency Management Plan is the entire written emergency plan. It consists of sub-plans covering preparedness (Emergency Management Plan, four priority common plans, hazard-specific preparedness plans) and recovery (service continuation).

Computer-Assisted Emergency Management refers to the use of personal computer-based software to assist an agency, business or government in many facets of emergency management. An increasing number of software packages are commercially available and usually focus on electronic logbooks, inventory and resource tracking, registration and inquiry, and facility management.

Concept of Operation is a concise and authoritative statement by an organization that precedes a planning endeavor. It states the organization's mission, the business/service functions critical to surviving an emergency and how it is envisioned these critical functions will be maintained. It forms the foundation for subsequent planning activities and provides general guidance on establishing planning priorities.

Council refers to the body elected to govern a local jurisdiction. This body may also be known as a Board, Commission, etc.

Critical Incident Stress Debriefing is a meeting of those affected by what they have encountered as an emergency occurs, is responded to, or is recovered from. It is facilitated by professional councillors and is intended to lessen the impact of major events on those affected and accelerate normal recovery in normal people after an abnormal event.

Critical Service Function is a service, function or operation performed by a local government that is essential to either maintain through the occurrence of an emergency or to immediately re-establish after an emergency occurs.

Detailed Evaluation is the second step of a three-step post-emergency building evaluation system (rapid, detailed, engineering evaluations). It is performed by a structural engineer and involves a complete visual inspection of the building.

Drill is one of the five types of exercises. It involves actual field response to test a single emergency response function.

Emergency is any present or imminent event that is caused by accident, fire, explosion or technical failure, or by the forces of nature, and requires prompt coordination of action or special regulation of persons or property to protect the health, safety or welfare of people or to limit damage to property.

Emergency Management Plan is the most important aspect of the Comprehensive Municipal Emergency Management Plan. It is the central document that conveys how all emergencies will be managed. Its generality is the key to its flexibility in that it touches only on those few critical management elements common to every emergency. One aspect covered in detail is the location, set up and operation of the Emergency Operations Center.

Emergency Program Coordinator is the person designated to facilitate the local government's emergency program. The Coordinator has two roles: planning and response. In the planning role the Coordinator works under the direction of the Emergency Program Planning Committee to facilitate construction of the Comprehensive Emergency Management Plan, training of personnel and exercises. In the response role the Coordinator has specific duties set out in the Plan in addition to acting as the expert advisor to those in the Emergency Operations Center. This function is also known as Emergency Planner, Contingency Planner, Disaster Preparedness Officer, Emergency Measures Officer, etc.

Emergency Program Planning Committee is the appointed standing body responsible for the ongoing management of the municipal emergency program. This includes planning, annual updates, training and exercising. The Committee typically includes a member of Council, Chief Administrative Officer, Emergency Program Coordinator, Fire Chief, Police Chief, medical representative, public works manager, Emergency Social Services Director and Telecommunications Officer.

Emergency Public Information Plan is one of the four common sub-plans that may be called upon if needed in any emergency. It details how information will be released to the media for dissemination to the public and who is responsible for ensuring such. Important elements of this plan are designation of a Public Information Officer and an Emergency Public Information Center.

Emergency Social Services Plan is one of the four common sub-plans that may be called upon if needed in any emergency. This plan details all aspects of caring for the human element affected by an emergency. It should include provisions for receiving evacuees, registration and inquiry and sheltering, feeding, clothing and counselling large numbers of people for extended periods.

Emergency Telecommunications Plan is one of the four common sub-plans that may be called upon if needed in any emergency. It assesses the vulnerability of existing systems and proposes alternatives that should ensure critical communications are maintained during an emergency.

Engineering Evaluation is the third step of a three-step post-emergency building evaluation system (Rapid, Detailed, Engineering Evaluations). It is performed by a consulting Structural Engineer retained by the building owner and involves consulting construction drawing, damage data and new structural calculations.

Evacuation Plan is one of the four common sub-plans that may be called upon if needed in any emergency. It identifies evacuation routes within and out of the community and details how residents are notified, how mobility impaired residents are moved, and security of the evacuated area. It should address two types of evacuation: immediate and anticipatory.

External Hazard refers to events occurring outside the local government's jurisdiction yet may have an impact on that community. For example, a major emergency in an adjacent community may require the secondment of expertise or equipment based on mutual aid agreements, or the receiving of evacuees. In this way emergencies affecting other communities have an indirect effect on your community.

Full-Scale Exercise is the largest and most involved of the five types of exercise. This type of exercise tests all aspects of a local government's emergency plan including policy, coordination, operations and field personnel.

Functional Exercise is one of the five types of exercise. It is an Emergency Operations Center exercise that involves the simulation of an emergency and time-sequenced messages to test the coordination and communication between participants. No field portion is associated with this type of exercise.

Geotechnical Hazard refers to ground movements either during or after an emergency. These can be either static, where the movement has already occurred resulting in surface fault rupture, or dynamic, where the movement is continuous such as mud or the settling of disturbed material.

Hazard refers to anything which either threatens the residents of a community or the things they value. From a municipal perspective this would include service delivery, infrastructure, civic facilities or anything that would generate a large number of evacuees or casualties.

Hazard-Specific Preparedness Plan is plan detailing preparedness for, and response to, an emergency caused by a specific hazard. Where the Emergency Management Plan sets out general emergency management procedures applicable to all emergencies, these plans are then relied on to provide specific detail unique to that hazard. It will include unique procedures, equipment and contacts. These plans make up the majority of the overall Comprehensive Emergency Management Plan.

Immediate Action Checklist is brief, point-form list of the most critical actions a responder must execute or consider in the first minutes of a response. These are applicable to any level of responder within a local government although they are most often used by senior managers stepping into an emergency management role. These serve as reminders of even the most obvious tasks since people's ability to focus is affected by a crisis and causes simple tasks to be overlooked.

Incident Command System (ICS) is an emergency management system specifically designed to allow its users to adopt an integrated organizational structure equal to the complexity and demands of single or multiple incidents without being hindered by jurisdictional boundaries.

Inspected is one of three building safety evaluation classifications (Inspected, Limited Entry, Unsafe). "Inspected" means no apparent hazard has been found and there is no restriction on use or occupancy.

Internal Hazard is a hazard endemic to a community. These may be natural hazards, human-caused hazards or social hazards. These categories encompass a range of potential emergencies that may befall a community and should, therefore, have preparedness plans written in advance.

Limited Entry is one of three building safety evaluation classifications (Inspected, Limited Entry, Unsafe). "Limited Entry" means a dangerous condition is believed to be present although entry by owner for emergency purposes only and at own risk is permitted.

Line of Succession is the list of persons designated to fulfill the role of Emergency Program Coordinator if he/she is unavailable or incapacitated.

Liquefaction is loss of stability in a load bearing soil as a result of vertical and/or horizontal ground motion and the water content of the soil.

Local Government is considered that level of government which is responsible for the provision of one or more services directly to residents of a defined, yet geographically limited, area. It may include villages, towns, cities, counties, regional districts, district municipalities, improvement districts, etc.

Mitigation is the first of the four phases of *Comprehensive Emergency Management*. It is the process by which the impact of potential emergencies may be reduced, deflected or avoided altogether.

Maximum Tolerable Disruption Time (MTDT) is a model used in Service Continuation Planning for determining the length of time a municipal function may out of service and assists in prioritizing critical service functions.

Mutual Aid Agreement is an agreement for support negotiated between two, usually neighboring, jurisdictions. These may exist for a number of departments (police, fire, ambulance, public works, emergency social services) and cover supplies, equipment, facilities and staff.

Non-Structural Hazard refers to the non-structural elements of a damaged building which may pose a hazard during and after an emergency. These would include parapets, canopies, external fixtures, glazing, curtain walls, ceiling fixtures, elevated fixtures, and elevators.

Orientation Seminar is the most basic of the five types of exercise. It is used to introduce or refresh participants to plans and procedures. It is usually delivered by lecture, panel discussion or talk-throughs.

Packet Radio is digital (computer to computer) communications over Amateur Radio frequencies. It is an excellent means of communicating lists of names and resources.

PHTO Model is the Physical, Human, Technology and Operations Model which is used to identify and assess the four essential elements of service delivery.

Planning Process is a logical, normative framework for guiding the evolution of ideas into implementable plans. It consists of identifying issues, evaluating them, developing a plan, analyzing it, implementing it, and then maintaining the plan.

Preparedness is the second and most involved of the four phases of *Comprehensive Emergency Management*. The preparedness phase is the opportunity to pre-plan for inevitable emergencies by providing procedures, checklists, resource information and contact information that will be urgently needed in the response to an emergency.

Preparedness Plan is the largest segment of the Comprehensive Municipal Emergency Plan. It includes the general Emergency Management Plan, the four common plans (emergency social services, Evacuation, Public Information, Telecommunications) and numerous hazard-specific preparedness plans.

Public Information Officer is the person responsible for the Emergency Public Information Plan and is the single point of contact at the local government for the media.

Public Works refers to the department of the local government that is responsible for the municipal infrastructure.

Rapid Evaluation is the first step of a three-step post-emergency building evaluation system (rapid, detailed, engineering evaluations). It is performed by qualified building inspectors, Civil/Structural Engineers or Architects and involves a rapid visual inspection of a building for any obvious compromise of safety and structural integrity. It is used to identify buildings requiring a detailed evaluation.

Reception Center is a facility established under the Emergency Social Services Plan. It is a suitable, usually public, facility that is available after an emergency to serve as a site for the registration of, and inquiry about, evacuees, as well as a shelter for those displaced by the emergency. Depending on the size of the community, more than one reception center may be established.

Recovery is the fourth and last phase of *Comprehensive Emergency Management*. It follows mitigation efforts, preparedness planning and actual emergency response. It involves specific plans to restore municipal services and infrastructure to pre-emergency levels. It is the largest phase of *Comprehensive Emergency Management*.

Registration and Inquiry is the process of establishing a central registry during an emergency where evacuees and other displaced persons must provide their name for tracking purposes. It is also the place to search for the location and status of such persons. This is usually co-located with a reception center.

Response is the third phase of *Comprehensive Emergency Management*. It is the time where planning activities undertaken in the preparedness phase are called upon. Well-prepared plans should unfold nearly automatically in the response phase.

Risk is the frequency of an identified hazard facing a community and the consequences that may result.

Risk Analysis is the process of evaluating the frequency and consequence of a hazard.

Risk Assessment is the estimating of the type and extent of impact from a known hazard.

Risk Control is a risk management technique that focuses on control measures, such as exposure avoidance, loss prevention, loss reduction, segregation of exposures and contractual transfer, to minimize potential losses.

Risk Financing is a risk management technique that accepts an exposure and pays for actual losses after an emergency by either retention, where the organization assumes financial responsibility, or through commercial insurance.

Risk Management is the weighing of the probabilities of an activity or activities leading to a consequence which has a negative impact on a community.

Service Continuation Plan is a Recovery Plan that addresses maintaining services as close to normal as possible, or restoring them in a prioritized yet timely manner after an emergency.

State of Local Emergency refers to the ability of a local government to declare such under Provincial or State legislation. It typically empowers a local government with extraordinary powers that includes the appropriation and expenditure of funds for emergency purposes. The ability to declare a state of local emergency, the process to do such and the powers it bestows will vary in each Province or State.

Tabletop Exercise is one of five types of exercises. It involves reviewing proposed actions to be taken in response to a described emergency situation and a series of messages to participants. It permits participants to practice problem solving for a coordinated, effective response.

Telecommunications is the collective name for all means of communication that rely on a form of electrical or mechanical support. It includes telephones, radios, facsimile, electronic data, etc.

Unsafe is one of three building safety evaluation classifications (inspected, limited entry, unsafe). "Unsafe" means an extreme hazard is present and a building is in imminent danger of collapsing.

VHF Radio is Very High Frequency Radio. It is a type of communications that employs frequency modulation (FM) on a certain band of the radio spectrum. It is commonly used by emergency services and public works and provides the most reliable radio communications for local government purposes.

Vulnerability Analysis follows risk analysis and risk assessment by estimating the impact of a hazard on specific elements of the community as a whole but also on the emergency response system.

Workplace Hazardous Materials Information System is a Canadian Federal statute requiring the identification of all hazardous materials in the workplace and mandatory minimum training for workers.

INDEX

F

G

H

ABOUT THE AUTHOR

JAMES A. GORDON holds a B.Sc. in Urban Geography and graduate degrees in Urban and Regional Planning and Public Administration. He is a Member of the Canadian Institute of Planners and a Fellow of the Institute of Chartered Secretaries and Administrators. He has been awarded the titles of *Professional Manager* by the Canadian Institute of Management and *Professional Administrator* by the ICSA. He is also a Certified Municipal Clerk and is certified in municipal administration by the Government of British Columbia.

Mr. Gordon has held senior management positions in two British Columbia local governments over the past six years. In addition to a wide range of corporate responsibilities, he has been active in local government emergency management as Program Coordinator and Deputy Coordinator. Prior to his local government career, Mr. Gordon was the Provincial Disaster Preparedness Coordinator for the British Columbia Ministry of Health.

Committed to life long learning, Mr. Gordon actively pursues professional development. This includes extensive training in risk and emergency management through courses at the Canadian Emergency Preparedness College and the Justice Institute of British Columbia, and with the Major Industrial Accident Council of Canada, the Canadian Society for Civil Engineering and the American Public Works Association. He has written on numerous subjects with risk and emergency management topics ranging from service continuation planning to wildland/urban interface fire protection.

In his spare time, Mr. Gordon is a licensed Amateur Radio operator and an Ironman triathlete. He has travelled widely in Asia, the South Pacific and North America, and enjoys reading adventure travel and geopolitics. He is married to a writer and lives in Kamloops, B.C., Canada.

ABOUT THE PUBLISHER

THE ROTHSTEIN CATALOG ON DISASTER RECOVERY

The industry's principal resource for 1,000+ books, software tools, videos and research reports, since 1989.

It is a division of **Rothstein Associates Inc.**, an international management consultancy focused on business continuity, crisis management, emergency management, risk mitigation and disaster recovery, since 1985.

The Rothstein Catalog On Disaster Recovery is also the principal publisher in the fields of Business Continuity, Disaster Recovery, and Service Level Agreements, with over 50 titles in print.

A complimentary CD-ROM will be sent upon request to: **info@rothstein.com**

www.rothstein.com
www.DisasterRecoveryBooks.com
www.ServiceLevelBooks.com
email: info@rothstein.com

www.rothstein.com

SELECTED TITLES FROM
THE ROTHSTEIN CATALOG
ON DISASTER RECOVERY

BUSINESS CONTINUITY: BEST PRACTICES by Andrew Hiles

"A practical implementation framework for the 10 core units of competence jointly established by the Disaster Recovery Institute International (DRII) and Business continuity Institute (BCI). It can be used as a step-by-step guide by those new to BC management or referred to by more seasoned professionals for ideas and updates on specific topics. The guide covers all units of competence decided upon by DRII and BCI, and adds further background based on the experience of the author. Examples are provided throughout the book -- all having their roots in real cases. It is intended to be updated regularly." - INFORMATION SECURITY MAGAZINE.

BCM FRAMEWORK™ CD: THE EASY-TO-USE, COMPREHENSIVE, CD-ROM-BASED BUSINESS CONTINUITY TOOL by Andrew Hiles

BCM FRAMEWORK represents a new approach in business continuity management software tools. The problem with a lot of software is that it is expensive; it requires training in use of the software; it may require consultancy in its use; it does not necessarily match your culture, requirements, or documentation standards; and, it still requires a lot of work to complete the detail, without which any disaster recovery plan is worthless.

    BCM FRAMEWORK consists of a number of easily tailored modules selected from our database of client work from a combined total of over one hundred years of consultancy experience - modules that are hand picked as the most relevant to your own situation, culture, organization, equipment platform and infrastructure. It contains Model Business Recovery Action Plans for key corporate functions with Organization Schematics and role descriptions, with some vital - and often forgotten - actions included.

BUSINESS EMERGENCY ACTION PLAN by Business_Policies.com

Federal and state Occupational Safety and Health Administration (OSHA) regulations require businesses to have a written Emergency Action Plan. The requirements for the plan include establishing responsibility for developing emergency evacuation routes, training personnel, designating assembly points for emergencies, and much more. This model Emergency Action Plan can be quickly modified to meet federal and state Occupational Safety and Health Administration (OSHA) requirements for each business to have a written plan in place. The model plan also includes guidelines to distribute and implement the plan to meet OSHA requirements.

BUSINESS THREAT AND RISK ASSESSMENT CHECKLIST
by Edmond D. Jones

This manual contains checklists that an individual or group may use to evaluate the threats and risks which may impact an organization's campus, facility or even specific departments within the organization. Each of the checklists shown in this manual and a cover page that may be used to assemble your own checklists are contained on the CD that accompanies this manual.